FuelForward

Discover Proven Practices to Fuel Your Career Forward

Vivian Hairston Blade

Parker House Publishing
ParkerHouseBooks.com

Production: ParkerHouseBooks.com
Printed and bound in the United States of America.

The web addresses referenced in this book were active and correct at the time of the book's publication but may be subject to change.

What people are saying . . .

I'm grateful Vivian reminds us that careers are neither static nor accidental; they require attention and action. You are most valuable when you develop your skills in broad areas while diving deep into your fields of interest. Stagnancy is NOT an option. If you need motivation and tactics to hone your calling, FuelForward is the tool for you!

Bethany Miller, MBA
Captain, UPS Airlines
Flight Operations Technical/Safety Supervisor

For those who want to jump-start their careers, FuelForward is a practical "field survival guide" to navigating the corporate ladder. Vivian lays out a crisp, thought-provoking approach to taking control of one's career, providing rich examples that stimulate and motivate.

Vivian builds a compelling case of how hard work alone is not sufficient in our current work environment to ensure success. She calls to the forefront the blind spots that can make or break advancement.

Vivian masterfully describes the new paradigm as "spiral advancement" versus the traditional "vertical corporate ladder." She encourages you to assess career moves as a succession of chess moves that build a strong toolkit of skills, strengths, and capabilities.

I highly recommend FuelForward for those who want to simply take their game to the next level.

Mark Shirkness
General Manager, Distribution & Service
General Electric

Vivian Blade has provided an outstanding body of work that is rich with real-time unwritten rules and examples that propel careers in today's ever-changing workplace. Her robust treatment includes challenging mindsets, understanding the principles of success, creating a solid foundation, and managing reputation, reach, and relationships.

Professionals hungry for success will learn first-hand how companies define top talent and how to stand out. It gives you a unique lens for learning directly from the success that senior leaders have had in their personal careers.

Interfacing with senior VPs weekly forces me to constantly manage my personal brand. As a mid-career professional, I especially appreciated the tips in Chapters 6 and 8 around reputation and relationships.

Mandisa M. Diggs
Inclusion & Collaboration HR Business Partner
Cisco Systems

Being in the business of helping hi-potential women accelerate their careers, I highly recommend Vivian Blade's book FuelForward. She helps you understand the fundamentals of not only building your career through hard work and effort (that's a given) but thoughtfully applying her model to strengthen your "runway" for success.

Sally Schott
President and Founder
Peer Exchange Network

FuelForward takes all the thought out of what's required to take your career to the next level. The author gives you a road map that's easily followed, setting you up for success you probably never knew you could achieve.

It's an easy read for those who want to advance not only in a career, but in life as well. The author keeps it real by featuring real-life experiences.

Once you pick it up, you won't put it down until you're done!

Charlette Fairchild, Ph.D.
National Accounts Manager
General Electric

Vivian Blade has written an insightful "playbook" for accelerating one's career. It's a must-read for all who seek to move up.

Building on one's career foundation of expertise, experience, and execution, Vivian carefully constructs the scaffolding of reputation, reach, and relationships to form the structure for accelerating your career.

Following the guidelines outlined in this "playbook" will result in a more fulfilling career delivered faster.

Allen Cawley
Chief Operating Officer
SOAR

Ms. Blade lays out a concise, thought-provoking roadmap for managing and accelerating one's career. Written in an easy-to-read style, anyone can benefit from the advice and examples portrayed—a must-read for anyone serious about advancing his or her career.

Lois Prytherch
Johnson & Johnson

FuelForward really captured the tools needed to navigate through ones career. Had I possessed these keys when I began my corporate climb 30 years ago, promotions would have come sooner and more frequently. The advice Vivian shares here is never outdated.

Although I'm well into my career, I'll take advantage and use the pointers from this book because they are still relevant.

D. Durell Hoskins
Area Sales Manager
General Electric

Dedication

My mother, Zada Stowe Hairston, went to work in the Head Start program when I was three years old. Over the years, she grew her career from the role of cook to assistant teacher to teacher. She always knew she could do more and always wanted to challenge herself to learn, grow, and be all that she could be. Education was important to her and my father, Elbert Hairston. They educated all seven of their children through college and advanced degrees. My mother went back to school to earn her associate degree. She set an example for us each and every day.

Though she didn't realize it during those years of hard work trying to support her family, her values helped her move into roles where she could influence the children, parents, and staff whose lives she touched on ever-deepening levels. Of utmost importance was the Christian spirit with which she served others, loving them no matter what their circumstances. Because of that, she built respectful, lifelong relationships.

My mother applied these principles—many of which I share with you in this book—to make a difference in her workplace, her church, and her community. It wasn't until years later when I made the connection between these values my mother had demonstrated throughout my life and the principles I would need to advance my career.

I dedicate this book to my mother, Zada Hairston, for being a role model to so many throughout her life.

Thank you, Mama. I love you!

Acknowledgments

I owe a great deal of thanks to several people who helped make *FuelForward* possible. First of all, my work with Johnson & Johnson in training professionals on career management helped me realize how important this topic is to help professionals succeed, and how little is known about how to advance careers. I realized there was an unfulfilled need for knowledge I could bring to countless professionals. I acknowledge Kelly Schmidt and Lois Prytherch for their partnership during that initial program.

Cathy Fyock, my writing coach, helped me stay on track and encouraged me to keep writing. Thank you for being there for me, and for sharing resources that could help me through each phase of the process. Joan Fox was my accountability partner in the early stages of the book. Friends Richard McKnight, Tracey Purifoy-Moneypenny, and Kimberly Black-Maffet provided early feedback and inspired me to succeed.

I thank those who participated in the research and interviews. I appreciate your willingness to share your time, experiences, and lessons learned. Your stories will help so many professionals achieve their career goals.

I also am grateful for my children, Alivia and Percy Blade, who were there to bounce ideas off and share their opinions.

My greatest appreciation goes to my husband, Vance Blade, who has supported my career aspirations from our earliest days together. You have been a blessing as a life partner, sharing in anything that needed to be done to make sure I could take advantage of every opportunity to succeed in my career. Thank you for your encouragement and ideas in writing this book.

Foreword

What does it take to make it to the top of the career ladder? Whether you start as a grocery bagger as I did or you dream of reaching the top of your profession, how can you make your career journey shift into overdrive? By following Vivian Blade's guidance in *FuelForward*. This book explores how to get to the next stop on your journey in such detail that you won't be left guessing what to do. In fact, you'll find yourself climbing rapidly *IF* you apply its foundation and accelerators to your own career.

I recently retired as president of a large division of The Kroger Co. after a work history that spanned five decades. Working for this giant grocery store chain, I both witnessed and experienced what it takes to achieve a rewarding top-level career. As you read *FuelForward*, you'll discover factors that most resonate with you. In my career at Kroger, five factors that meant a lot to me were 1) emphasizing the basics, 2) branding myself, 3) focusing on customer needs, 4) recognizing others along the way, and 5) working with mentors and sponsors.

The basics start with not having a sense of entitlement—a topic Vivian addresses well in *FuelForward*. She pulls no punches when she writes, "There *is* no entitlement. The company does not owe you a promotion. It's up to you to ensure your leaders know you are ready for added responsibility." Yet too many people want to start at third base and reach "home" without running around all the bases first. No company owes you more than a fair chance, and average isn't good enough.

Here's an example. Years ago, one of my associates wondered why I always gave her average ratings on her performance review. She never considered her performance to be average until she was told that "just doing your job" is average. I encouraged her to look for opportunities to excel and shared ways the person previously in this role had taken the initiative. That made an impression. Before long, she found ways to perform her job "above and beyond," and her higher rating reflected that.

Other critical basics to nail include the nonverbal image you convey in any job situation. Your first impression carries a lot of weight—your body language, attitude, and tone with which you speak to others. Are you walking your talk? Are you setting positive examples? Are you a team player? Are you dressing and grooming as a professional should? As my grandfather said, "There might be an excuse for being poor, but there's no excuse for being dirty." You can imagine how especially important that is for workers in the food business!

When it comes to branding oneself, I see it as building an intentional, not an accidental, reputation. I was known at Kroger as the guy who insisted floors were clean and no lines of people were waiting to check out. Employees knew that about me; it was part of my branding. So they paid extra attention to these factors when I visited (and, I hope, when I wasn't around, too).

Related to that, customer focus had my constant attention at Kroger. When we held an internal meeting, for example, we would strategically place a cardboard cutout of a lady customer at the table. We "consulted" her often in our discussions.

In addition, when it comes to accelerating their careers, leaders need to consider employee recognition every bit as much as customer focus. I'll never forget my first store manager who encouraged me to excel when I started at age seventeen. He would get on the store's PA system and praise me or another employee for winning a football game or earning straight A's or getting accepted into college. Customers heard this and stood in the aisles applauding. By his actions, he modeled the importance of praising others and letting us experience how good that recognition feels. It never fails; if you shine a light on someone, the afterglow shines back on you.

Another manager mentored me and several managers sponsored me to climb up the corporate ladder. In their roles of mentors and sponsors, they showed me how to stand out and be a leader. *FuelForward* puts a lot of emphasis on finding mentors and sponsors by building strong relationships along the way. Referring often to their importance, Vivian's guidance is right on target. Don't underestimate the importance of these valuable management connections!

Vivian "gets it" because she has lived it. I have personally watched her career develop as she journeyed to where she is today. Her vast experiences with Fortune 100 companies in various positions have qualified her to lay out the strategies for building your road map to success. Using this book, you can confidently apply her concepts and tools at any point during your career—and excel as a result.

I encourage you to take to heart Vivian Blade's words of wisdom as you soar to new heights on your career journey.

John Hackett
Past President, Mid-South Division
The Kroger Co.

Table of Contents

Introduction

Hungry for Success?

Have you ever seen change before like you see it today? Everything around us changes as quickly as a chameleon changes colors. The workplace is especially vulnerable to change. In recent years, economic pressures and generational influences have radically changed the face of the places we call work.

The effects of downsizing have taken many professional careers down unexpected paths. The types of jobs and skills needed in today's economy have evolved.

The 21st century has given us the gift of four generations in the workplace at one time. The effect on organizational culture is unprecedented. What is acceptable today, as it relates to careers, was frowned upon just a few years ago.

The way we define a career has been turned on its head. Instead of working for a single company for 35 years, professionals may work for as many as five or more companies during that same time. The ritual of having to "pay your dues" is considered a thing of the past. Professionals expect to be promoted much more quickly than before. They have little patience for a long climb up the corporate ladder.

For companies, the cost of this new career environment hits hard. Their workforce has a variety of career expectations that must be given attention. And shorter tenures often force companies into a vicious cycle of recruiting, hiring, and training. These effects cost companies directly in cash and indirectly in lost productivity, loss of institutional knowledge, and declines in employee engagement. They can't afford to ignore the consequences of the new normal. In response, their strategy must focus on helping employees feel connected to the organization in a meaningful way and feel they have the potential to achieve their career goals.

This new career environment poses challenges for professionals as well. For example, a career move that you haven't strategically planned for may not move you forward. You may find yourself bouncing around to find the right opportunity, only to find yourself moving but not growing.

Managing your career is an essential skill to master, or you risk falling behind. How can professionals thrive in this maze of seemingly endless change that has become the new norm? How can company leaders create a more stable and productive work force when "loyalty" seems to have lost its meaning? How can you, as a professional, continue to gain momentum in your career when the "career game" seems daunting, and the future is so uncertain?

Not everyone wants to be the CEO or even vice president. However, everyone wants to be recognized and rewarded for good work. For many professionals, this means getting promoted and seeing their careers move ahead. There's an opportunity for both sides—employer and employee—to work together in employee career management in ways that can benefit each party.

Keep Perspective of Balance in Mind

If you are a leader who has a passion to create an engaged and successful organization, be sure to read this book. Become aware of the dynamics of career management that are sometimes not obvious but still directly influence the professionals on your team. Your awareness will also allow you to create a more balanced and supportive environment when it comes to helping employees succeed. Read this book with that perspective in mind. Consider what you can do to make a difference for professionals' careers in your organization. When your employees succeed, you succeed.

One Fortune 50 company has seen the difference the training on these career skills has made on its organization. As one expert I interviewed, Kelly Schmidt from Johnson & Johnson, said:

> I think there are two things that come from it. From an engagement perspective of our team, we're seeing people are focused more on their personal development and how they can grow in a more concerted fashion. From a business perspective, I think we'll see that people are better engaged with understanding the business. So if you're managing your career a little differently, part of that is focusing on relationships. If you have better relationships built, you'll start understanding the business a bit better and can be considered a better business partner. It's not as overt as the development activities and the personal impact, but overall I think if you have better relationships, obviously you'll have better business results.

Your company may be experiencing higher turnover rates among some of your best talent. This book will help you create an environment in which employees feel valued and can more comfortably share their value. You'll find this is required to gain career momentum.

Your company may be missing opportunities for some of your best talent to show what they can do. This book will help you understand how a culture of informal and formal systems assists your greatest talent in becoming visible. As a result, it can have an even greater effect on your business results.

Who Should Read *FuelForward*?

If you are a professional with a hunger for success, you need to read this book.

You may be a professional at mid-career trying to weave your way into a management role. This book will help you come out of the woodwork and get on the radar screen of decision makers.

You may be a professional who has significant management experience and wants to reach the next level of leadership. This book will help you gain the credibility you need to be seen as a serious contender for a significant role.

You may be a professional who's been working in individual contributor roles. This book will help you leverage the assets you bring to the table to open new opportunities at this stage of your career.

You may be a professional who expects your career path to move quickly across companies. This book will help you benefit from each step so you can be seen as the asset the next company is seeking.

As you read *FuelForward*, it will require some work from you. I'll challenge your thinking and courage. I'll ask you to take a candid look in the mirror and be honest with yourself about what you see. You'll reflect on your current and past situations to illuminate your experiences and enlighten your perspective. You'll have to get out of your comfort zone and do things a little differently in order to get different results.

This book will provide a framework that will be your road map for career success. If you'd like more structured support along the way, feel free to reach out to me. My passion is working with professionals to help them realize success.

I challenge you to see just how far you can go.

On your mark, get set . . .

Meet the Professionals Interviewed for *FuelForward*

I completed two types of research to prepare for this book. First, I administered a quantitative survey to professionals with at least a college degree and professional work experience. Then, I held a series of interviews with professionals at various stages of their careers. You'll hear about their career experiences and perspectives on the factors that will help you FuelForward.

Let's meet the professionals featured throughout this book.

Rita M. Barksdale

Rita is a general manager at GE Healthcare. She has nearly 20 years of professional and leadership experience with GE, growing her career from a technical leadership program member to an executive leader of a GE business unit.

Kimberly Black-Maffet

Kimberly serves as associate athletic director at the University of Louisville. In her career, she spent her early years in healthcare as a practitioner and a leader before moving into higher education and athletics.

Ralph de Chabert

Ralph is the chief diversity officer for the Brown-Forman Corporation. He has gained experience in a variety of industries while maintaining a focus on a specific technical area. Ralph has spent the past 20 years of his career in senior-level roles.

Katie Gaughan

Katie is president and founder of Point C Business Consultancy. Most of her career centered on marketing. She has spent the past several years running her own business as an executive coach and leadership development professional.

Jeff Nally

Jeff is an executive coach and coaching practice leader for a Fortune 100 healthcare and well-being company. Through his roles in the fields of human resources and organizational development, he has developed a deep skillset that has been transferable across industries.

Tracey Purifoy-Moneypenny

Tracey is a director at a higher education institution. Her career accelerated through individual contributor and management roles in the marketing industry. She found a passion for higher education and quickly earned the lead role at a satellite campus.

Kelly Schmidt

Kelly serves as an IT director with Johnson & Johnson. Her career has advanced over the years in roles across business units within the same company. Her experience in individual contributor roles helped her prepare for increasingly responsible leadership positions within IT.

Melanie Shook

Melanie is the vice president of customer experience at Neustar, Inc. She built a career with deep expertise in call center operations. Her leadership experience has been an interesting journey spanning a variety of industries.

Nancy Torra

Nancy serves as a project manager for a Fortune 100 healthcare and well-being company. Her career has been an interesting mix of individual contributor and manager roles within the same company. This path has given her a rich depth of industry experience in healthcare.

Chapter One

Does Hard Work Pay Off?

Throughout your life, you've been raised with the principle that if you work hard, you can do anything. Your hard work will pay off with success. Does hard work pay off?

For the college athlete who constantly conditions and practices, makes it into professional sports, and eventually leads his team to the national title, most would say, "Hard work pays off." For the avid gardener who carefully tends his landscaping to create a picture-perfect yard that neighbors envy, most would say, "Hard work pays off." For the small business owner who spends countless hours working to make the company profitable until she opens her second location, most would say, "Hard work pays off." For the hikers who, after enduring grueling conditions, finally make it to the mountain summit on their third attempt, most would say, "Hard work pays off."

We see and hear about many examples convincing us that, yes, hard work does pay off. How would you answer this question for yourself? In your life experiences, has hard work paid off? What examples can you think of in which working hard has paid off for you?

Now, consider this question in terms of the effect that hard work has had on your career. When you think about how your career has progressed, would you say, "Hard work pays off?"

You probably would agree that, yes, you do work hard. You feel like there are never enough hours in the day to get everything on your to-do list completed. You spend countless hours at work. You plug in when you get home. You get up the next morning and do it all over again. To survive or progress, you've got to work hard.

However, can you actually *see the payoff* for all that hard work? Not so sure? Do you often find yourself frustrated when you labor yet fail to advance in your career as you had hoped?

Why does hard work not pay off the way you expect it to in the career area of your life?

What Does It Take to Get Ahead?

Have you ever had a conversation with a friend or co-worker that sounds like this: "Why, when I come in early, stay late, and do the things my manager or the organization has asked me to do, I still don't get promoted? What else does it take?"

You, like many other professionals, may share this sentiment. As I talk to people about their careers and the challenges they face, I hear this one the most. You feel like you're working hard and doing the right things, but you're *having the same discussion* with your manager the next year again. Your manager says, "You're doing great! Just keep working hard and work on these things." And with a symbolic pat on the head, you're encouraged to hang in there.

Yet people sincerely want to solve the puzzle of *how to get ahead*. But they're perplexed with questions such as these:

"If I'm doing what I think I'm supposed to be doing, why isn't it working?"

"Why did she get promoted ahead of me?"

"What am I missing? How does the game really work?"

"Are my expectations unrealistic?"

"Am I just not good enough?"

There seem to be no clear answers. "Keep working hard and talk to your manager" is the common refrain.

Different Challenges Today

Today's environment also brings different challenges than in the past. Professionals are often expected to change companies and industries to round out their career experiences and path. So I also hear discussions about how to effectively navigate those career moves. Many of the same challenges exist for either internal or external career progression.

In small to mid-sized companies, some of the same unsettling feelings and concerns surface about career advancement. Small companies tend to have a flat organizational structure, which limits the number of available opportunities to advance. Therefore, people feel the need to move to other companies or industries to advance their career. While at these small companies, you may tend to have broad responsibilities, which can be an advantage in your personal development and marketability. But how will that experience ultimately help you get ahead?

With these uncertainties, frustrations, and questions stirring in your mind, you simply want answers.

What Does Progress Take Besides Hard Work?

When it comes to career advice, professionals have been swimming in an environment of sameness. "Just focus on your job and work hard every day. You'll eventually get noticed and get promoted." Some professionals have a hard time getting beyond this engrained concept: *Work ethic is the measure of dedication and commitment to the job.* Thus, this subjective metric becomes the yardstick to compare one person's effort to another's, one person's work to another's.

Some of the greatest leadership gurus and CEOs agree that dedication and hard work definitely influence career. They believe these qualities are fundamental "must haves." For example, during a Women in the Economy conference it hosted, *The Wall Street Journal* reported that former CEO of General Electric Jack Welch said, "To get ahead, focus laser-like on performance . . . raise your hand for line jobs and tough, risky assignments."

But this traditional paradigm of hard work *alone* is insufficient. Leadership gurus and executives also talk about other hidden influences that, in addition to hard work, accelerate your progress.

In interviews with 11 women CEOs of Fortune 500 companies, *The Wall Street Journal* reporter John Bussey asked these leaders about the factors that fueled their careers. Most notably, they agreed with Welch in taking on tough assignments to prove their ability to execute and gain critical skills that will pay off in future roles. From there, the advice differed around issues of career planning, decision-making, image, mentoring, and alliances.

Sometimes, hidden influences on career advancement are blind spots both women and men fail to realize are steadily working in the background. Whether moving across companies or climbing the career ladder in your current organization, you can tap into a fundamental set of principles at work to move your career forward.

12

In Search of Answers

In addition to a national discussion sparked at the Women in the Economy event, the corporate environment has experienced a wave of interest in understanding these career-influencing principles.

Two Fortune 500 companies contacted me within weeks of each other, each seeking a training program on career management concepts. Their interest was much the same as the buzz in the news—that is, these companies wanted their employees to be aware of the layers of career management and feel empowered to manage their own careers. In addition, interest continues to surface from the articles I've written on this topic. Professionals attending the leadership programs I facilitate face these same concerns about career management.

I set out to uncover the truths about how to get ahead in your career. What's the inside scoop on what really happens? What's behind the advice from these CEOs and leadership experts? What pictures would professionals paint from their experiences? How would the uniqueness of one person's story reveal lessons that could translate into strategies to help countless others?

I wanted to get into the depths of the stories that paint the experiences of both male and female professionals. I wanted to uncover the lessons people learn but don't readily talk about. I wanted to hear about their triumphs, trials, and traps to watch out for. Most important, I sought to learn how these professionals were empowered to achieve the career goals that were most important in their lives.

I found the truths I was searching for. Through research and a series of interviews, I've discovered what makes real progress happen. Has much changed in the past 20 years? Yes, careers have changed as the economic and social environment has changed. But, to my surprise, I found cases in which the more things changed, the more they stayed the same!

For example, I found continued frustration, yet strength and perseverance, among professional women who are breaking through the layers of the glass ceiling. I discovered unspoken and unwritten rules still exist. Several men I interviewed revealed important tips that aren't taught beyond the typical advice of "keep your head down and work hard." These influential tips affect the careers of both genders. They're often intangible, thus not easy to pinpoint or explain. So often, they're not even discussed.

I did learn today's workplace is still driven by the relationships and connections people build. Through the experiences these professionals shared, you'll see how.

Eye-opening Insights

As you move up in your career, the rules of engagement often shift at different levels. This book will open your eyes to the realities of what it takes to manage your career and reach your goals. You'll also discover strategies and tools to make the tactics of career management easier, empowering you to FuelForward.

Get ready to make changes to achieve your career goals. Successful people are always learning and improving themselves. So, be open to new ideas, test the strategies, and use the tools at your disposal. Even if these concepts are familiar to you, I ask that you look at them with a fresh perspective.

Take a close look in the mirror. Be honest with yourself about your personal and professional goals, where you are in the process, and what you need to do to achieve what's important to you.

As you learn about the career success practices through this book, you'll identify areas of focus to help you FuelForward. You'll avoid the frustration and regret of realizing years later that your career ladder was a longer, higher climb than you expected.

●   ●   ●

REMEMBER:

⇒ The traditional paradigm of hard work *alone* is not sufficient to FuelForward in today's environment.

⇒ Leaders speak of hidden influences that, in addition to hard work, fuel your career forward. They can become blind spots for professionals who want to advance.

⇒ As you read this book, honestly reflect on your goals and your progress. Be open to strategies you can apply to achieve success as you define it.

Does Hard Work Pay Off?

Chapter Two

Careers: A Mindset

The Amazing Race

If you've ever seen the television show *The Amazing Race*, then you've experienced the adventure of the competing teams in their quest to be the first to finish the race.

The teams receive a challenge to complete a journey around the world. In each leg of the race, teams finish a task that allows them to move to the next leg. They have to come up with strategies, use and acquire resources, and work through challenges that surface along the way. Though on the same mission as every other, each team has a different race experience, influenced by the decisions and strategies it believes will help it succeed. Even though the ultimate goal is to be the first team to reach the finish line, the experience of getting to that point differs for each team.

A career can feel like *The Amazing Race*, full of competition with others in the organization pursuing the same upper levels in a company's hierarchy. You move along your career path completing goals, gaining skills and experience in each leg of your journey. Even though your career path may be similar to others' in terms of stops along the way, what you experience will be decidedly different from theirs.

No two careers are alike. No two people have exactly the same career aspirations or experiences. Many factors influence a person's career desires and decisions.

A career is not a static destination. You don't just land there and call it done. Successful people are always challenging themselves to reach further into the unknown. They are flexible as the world around them changes.

A career is an active endeavor—something you make happen, not something that happens to you. Think of it as a journey moving along a path that's mapped out ahead of time and then adjusted along the way. It's a series of short-term milestones that, when pieced together, form a trail you travel over a course of many years. You chase the goals of a particular job for a short time, but you pursue a career over the long haul.

Do you remember the classic movie *The Wizard of Oz*? The young girl Dorothy, the Lion, the Tin Man, and the Scarecrow went on a journey. These characters progressed along the yellow brick road overcoming challenges as they sought to acquire the character traits they felt they were missing. The Scarecrow wanted a brain to improve his wisdom. The Tin Man wanted a heart to feel and give compassion. The Lion wanted to be brave and have courage. Dorothy wanted to find her way back home to Kansas. So they traveled on the yellow brick road looking for what each of them needed to find.

As you move along *your* yellow brick road, you'll pass through milestones and expand your leadership, interpersonal, and technical skills in each leg. Remember, a career is never a straight path to the finish line nor a single destination. *It's your journey to Oz!*

A Career Is—

A career may take different twists and turns, some planned and some unplanned. If you have an idea where you want your career path to go, many of your twists and turns will likely be planned, giving you more control over where you'll end up. Planning gives you the opportunity to assess which paths best help you on your journey.

Sometimes the optimal career path will lead you to roles that are horizontal within an organization instead of vertical leading upward. At times, you may need to deepen your experience by taking roles outside of your current function, business unit, or even company.

Among the professionals I interviewed, career paths sometimes took unexpected turns. In some cases, they moved unexpectedly to a different industry. For example, a career that began in healthcare led to a leadership role in collegiate sports administration. A career in banking led to a leadership role in higher education. A rising star in mid-career decided to take a lateral move to get experience in more than one product line. Leaders being groomed for executive roles are often placed in lateral functional roles to gain experience and learn how different functions or business units influence the entire operation.

Given the vision and goals they had set for themselves, the types of roles these professionals stepped into were available to them because they had developed their skill sets and built important relationships. They accumulated wisdom, courage, and passion. As a result, they drew the attention of other leaders who believed in their abilities, both inside and outside their organizations.

Through meaningful experiences, you can increase your value to the business. You also gain courage or confidence in yourself, both in your technical abilities and your capacity to lead. Your depth in the business gives you more heart for what you do and the people you work with. You become wiser and better able to make sound decisions because you have increased awareness of the effects of your decisions. This can also increase the trust people have in you *and* their respect for your ability to lead.

A Changing Work Environment

As the latest generations have entered the workforce, the work environment has changed. What things have had the most effect on career advancement?

One is the degree of loyalty employees have to a company over the life of their careers, and vice versa. Professionals expect to change companies to gain experience that will move their careers ahead. Companies also want to have greater flexibility in the composition of their teams. My survey respondents noted that technology has changed the locations where we work and how we engage with fellow employees. Therefore, it has become more challenging than ever to find opportunities to build relationships, gain visibility, and grow careers.

Jeff Nally, an executive coach and coaching practice leader for a Fortune 100 healthcare and well-being company, talked about how he's seen definite changes emerge.

> It's not just the promotion along the hierarchy that is the only way to advance. It's moving broadly across the organization or across the professions and industries, or taking a stairstep approach to advancement. Today, it's not the traditional ascent in the organization chart that we are probably familiar with and have been clear about in the past.

Currently, it's common for a career path to move across companies—whether by choice or not. If it's your choice to move, make sure you don't make the jump just because you think the grass is greener on the other side. Once you get there and have an inside view, you realize it's not as green as it looked. So, be thoughtful in your considerations for these moves. Do your best to discern which opportunities will best fulfill your professional and personal goals.

A Plan, Not a Prayer

If you've ever watched *The Amazing Race*, then you know the incredible tasks the teams have to complete to reach the next milestone. Each leg of the race is difficult and time sensitive. Without careful planning, coordination, and tenacity, a team can lose ground and risk elimination. Team members have to keep the vision of the end game front and center. This vision motivates them to be strategic in their decisions, stay the course, and push through the obstacles they encounter. How much do they want to win?

Like the teams in *The Amazing Race*, you'll progress if you have a vision of what you want in life and the person you want to become. Without vision and a sense of direction, you may end up in roles that add little value to achieving your goals.

For example, Karen was a mid-level manager working in a Six Sigma quality role when she was considering her next job move. Opportunities included roles in an area that was becoming a new strategic priority for the company. She thought this lateral career move would help her gain new experience for the future.

But Karen had not taken the time to carefully weigh the experiences and skill sets she would acquire from this and other potential roles. She didn't ask which position would be the best for her career in the long run. As a result, jumping into this new, high-profile department actually put her career behind a couple of years.

During my discussion with Jeff Nally, I asked him to go a little deeper in explaining his earlier comments on what career paths look like today and how to deal with the new paradigm. Here are the points he considers most important:

> I encourage professionals to craft their aspiration, to know themselves well enough to craft the story to what they think their aspiration looks like, where they want to go, and what they want to do—even if they don't know the organization or the job title. So craft the aspiration.
>
> The next thing is to think about spiral advancement instead of an advancement that looks more vertical in the organization chart. Many people move their career forward by thinking in a spiral, or a web, or a latticework instead of a direct vertical move up the org chart.
>
> You've got to keep growing and learning and flexing. Industries change and markets change. You change too. So, where is it you want to grow? Where is it you want to *learn* next, not just *work* next? And how can you be flexible and shift as industries shift or as you change in what you aspire to? Grow, learn, and flex.

Marking Milestones

A career is not just a series of seats you mark time in or move through aimlessly like musical chairs. Each stop in your career path is a point that marks a milestone in your growth.

Do you remember learning how to drive through a series of steps and milestones? At each one, you gain skills that help you at the next stage. The first lessons come before you ever turn on the car. Then, the lessons progress to driving straight ahead, backing up, parallel parking, taking the car on the highway, and so on. Your skill and confidence build at each stage until you're ready to take the road test.

At each stage in your career, you're contributing to the business while developing the tools and confidence to become a positive influence on both the business results and the people around you.

Consider This:

As you work on your career planning, ask these questions to help you map your journey:

- Which opportunities will allow me to use and build on my strengths?
- Will this role help me build the skills I need to further develop?
- What significant contributions can I make to the business in this role?
- Is this an opportunity to demonstrate and further develop my technical and leadership capabilities?
- How will this role help me prepare for future roles I'd like to move into?

Motivation to Succeed

When I was growing up, my father would always say, "Plan your work and work your plan." Career management requires focused effort. You have to carve out time to thoughtfully consider the possibilities for achieving your personal and professional goals. Then you have to commit yourself to working your plan. Without a connection to the things that motivate you, there's little hope or drive for putting in the hard work it takes to achieve the things that are important to you. These motivations influence the achievement of your life's work, both personally and professionally.

Have you ever tried to lose weight? To successfully lose weight and keep it off, you have to change your eating habits or increase your exercise—or ideally, both. Long-term success means changing your lifestyle, which can be significant. You have to be highly motivated by either intrinsic or extrinsic factors to stick it out and make lifelong adjustments.

What drives you (or people you know) to stay on course? Maybe you want to fit into that dress or suit for a special event, or you have health concerns, or you simply want to look or feel better. Whatever your reason, it's got to be compelling enough so you stick with it.

Set up strong motivators to push you toward your professional goals. Professional motivators are driven by both intrinsic and extrinsic factors and, as related to your work, can be categorized into five important areas:

1. **Values:** What are my values, the character traits that steer my moral compass? How do they align with the company's values?

2. **Vision/Personal Goals and Aspirations:** What things are most important in my life? What are my priorities? How do I define success, both personally and professionally? Can I achieve these on my current or desired path?

3. **Having Purpose:** What's my life's work? What purpose do my professional contributions serve? How do I fulfill it personally and professionally?

4. **Feeling Valued and Appreciated:** Am I contributing to something meaningful? How do I feel about my work? Are my contributions recognized? Do I believe I am compensated fairly?

5. **Hope for Future Fulfillment:** Where do I want to be in one to two years, five years, and 10 years, both personally and professionally?

Spend time reflecting on these questions, as your motivations hugely influence your sense of accomplishment and connection to your work. Be aware that, as your life changes, your motivations and the answers to these questions will evolve over time. Pinpoint what motivates you and revisit these questions periodically. You may need to call on them to help keep you moving forward.

Consider This:

What motivates you in your personal life and career?
- Values
- Vision / personal goals and aspirations
- Having purpose
- Feeling valued and appreciated
- Hope for future fulfillment

Along the way, evaluate whether your current employer, job and your career path align with your values, your priorities, and your aspirations.

When your personal motivations are attuned to the mission, vision, and values of the company, you become energized and more committed. You can become the leader the business needs to meet its goals, and you can be personally fulfilled. Who wants to feel stuck in a rut of routinely going to work every day? You have to feel like your values mesh as if you are fulfilling a purpose for the organization, for customers, and for yourself.

Career management takes commitment, focus, and tenacity. If your priorities are not clear and your motivation becomes weak, it's easy to fall behind.

● ● ●

REMEMBER:

$\Rightarrow$ A career is a nonlinear journey. You define the destination milestones across your career.

$\Rightarrow$ A career takes planning and consistent, focused effort if you want to succeed.

$\Rightarrow$ Identify the intrinsic and extrinsic factors that are most important to you. They will serve as motivators in achieving your goals.

Chapter Three

The FuelForward Model for Career Success

We continue to struggle with the notion of merit, wanting to believe that's real. And we want folks to believe that positions are earned through dint of sheer effort, i.e., people grow in an organization because they were rewarded solely for the results achieved through their hard work—I got this position because I earned it.

And it's true that they do work hard and they've done very, very well. But there also are these other elements that matter such as your ability to manage the unwritten rules. And the question is, "How do you find out about the unwritten rules?" Well, often you learn by violating one.

The problem is that depending on what the unwritten rule is, you could have your career derailed. Sometimes people find out about those unwritten rules because someone cares enough to pull them aside and give them a heads up. Typically, that happens because of another positive exposure you've had to that individual.

–Ralph de Chabert, Chief Diversity Officer
Brown-Forman Corporation

Importance of Career Management

Why is career management a big deal anyway? The answers are based on your personal goals and the relationship of your role to the objectives of the company. Let's explore this further.

Companies have two primary goals driving their ability to compete and grow. First is to add real value to the success their customers are trying to achieve, to be problem solvers and enablers in helping them. Second, companies strive to be perceived as valued and trusted partners that their customers can count on.

Companies need every employee to be on board with their business goals as they contribute to the company's success. This requires employees skilled in their areas of technical expertise to be leaders in owning the company's goals, and to be committed to doing what it takes to achieve those goals.

As companies grow, the number of employees often increases. So does the complexity of the organizational structure. More jobs exist on the front line. Naturally, the funnel gets smaller as you move up the food chain to higher levels on the organizational chart. Companies require capable, trusted operational and strategic leadership at each level, with the stakes for talent highest at the uppermost levels.

With greater scale and complexity comes the need to have systems and processes in place to manage that talent development and talent placement process. For example, at General Electric (GE), this process is called Session C.

GE is comprised of several businesses in a variety of industries. Each sub-business operates as a business unit. Starting at the lowest levels of a GE business unit's org chart, department leaders evaluate their talent through an annual performance review and ranking process. Managers highlight their department's top performers in meeting goals, demonstrating functional competencies, and living the company's values.

Talent assessments roll up from departments to functions to business units. The top talent across the organization is highlighted in a review with senior leaders within the business unit. An even narrower, senior-level talent review is held with GE's CEO.

Through this process, GE identifies high-potential talent. Some are added to a watch list indicating how they perform, lead, and handle themselves. Senior leaders may sponsor an identified talent as they become familiar with that person's potential. Some high-potential talent may even be put in roles to test their ability to lead in a variety of situations.

This process begins at the early stages of one's career so the company leaders have time to watch promising professionals and even influence their development and career paths for future roles. This process is not unique to GE. Many companies have a defined approach to discovering and nurturing high-potential professionals.

They don't get on the talent watch list by accident. Companies are hiring people who have or can develop the skill sets to do the job. What do identified high-potential talents do? They take the initiative to differentiate their level of execution and build connections with other professionals and leaders. They become known as serious players on the company's team.

While the process just described funnels talent visibility to high levels of the company, the functional reviews throughout this process drive much of the mid-level talent movement as well. So, while your goal may not be to become a vice president or CEO, the same basic principles are still at work at all levels of the organization.

In small- to mid-size companies, the processes for talent development and progression may be less formal than described. But they're no less important. Small companies can be more vulnerable than large ones if they fail to have the right talent in the right seat on the team. Small business owners and leaders are watching the abilities and engagement of their employees. They know who can handle broadened responsibilities and whom they can trust to follow through.

Whether you realize it or not, talent assessments and decisions are constantly being made.

FuelForward Career Success Principles

How can you participate in this career-progressing process? Let's start with an understanding of two fundamental principles that drive career progression:

1) Building Your Foundation
2) Engaging Accelerators

These two principles comprise the basis of the Career FuelForward Model.

If you were a bodybuilder, how would you prepare for a lifting competition? To lift great amounts of weight, you must first build a strong core because your physical ability works together as a system. Your core provides the base of your strength. Your arm and leg muscles give you specific capacity to execute different types of lifts. You then focus your development based on how you wish to compete and your goals.

Similarly, to have a successful professional career requires working on your core—your foundation—first. Then you add strategies that have high probabilities for successful outcomes. As you gain acceleration, you optimize your chances for driving your career exactly as you want it.

Principles that Drive Career Progression
Career FuelForward Model

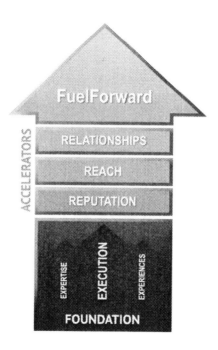

The *FuelForward* principles of career success first involve *building the foundation* of your skills and experience—your core. That will allow you to contribute superior levels of execution and positively affect your organization's success. To progress means *engaging the accelerators* that will help you energize the momentum toward your career goals.

33

Therefore, both Building Your Foundation and Engaging Accelerators are critical, complementary strategies to work on.

Building Your Foundation
- Expertise
- Experiences
- Execution

Your foundation, the basis on which everything in your career is built, is an area over which you have the most control. A strong foundation means having a meaningful base of knowledge, skills, and experiences—one that lets you add value to the organization through solid, consistent execution.

This foundation includes educational background, technical skills, leadership skills, value system, personal accountability, work ethic, emotional intelligence, organizational acumen, and work experiences where these characteristics develop. Respondents to my survey frequently reported that developing skills through education and training, combined with a strong work ethic, would contribute to the solid execution needed to advance.

A surprising number of respondents stressed the importance of going beyond an undergraduate degree to earn an advanced degree. Research supports this advice. According to the U.S. Census Bureau and many other studies, people with advanced degrees earn more money and have a greater number of opportunities available to them over the course of their careers.[i] [ii] [iii]

Because organizations have to deliver for customers, stockholders, and stakeholders, having employees who can get the job done is paramount. Organizations evaluate you on your ability to do the work. "What has she contributed consistently?" Then, they look at *how* the job gets done—your leadership and interpersonal style. "How well does she work with others?" They also consider your potential to do what's required effectively.

The foundation that you build affects your ability to deliver high quality work, but it's not a one-time activity. Like a bodybuilder, the stronger the foundation built within the core, the greater the ability to lift and compete. This requires continuous training and focus on the base to optimize the power delivered in lifts.

As you progress in your career, your skills will develop, the requirements for your role will evolve, and expectations will increase. The skills and expectations for professionals early in their careers differ from those of a mid-level professional or leader. In the short term, you want to recognize the most important performance expectations and required skills in your current job. Also, look ahead at the roles on your desired career path and determine the skills and experiences required for success as you progress. Proactively look for opportunities to build those skills along the way.

Continuing to strengthen your foundation influences your ability to both handle and be ready for greater responsibility.

Consider This:

What have you done today to add value in your execution of responsibilities? This is the mantra for Building Your Foundation. List one or two ways you've added value today.

Engaging the FuelForward Accelerators
- Reputation (Personal Brand)
- Reach (Broadened Connections)
- Professional Relationships (Allies and Advocates)

As you establish a solid foundation and a reputation for getting the job done, simultaneously work on engaging the FuelForward Accelerators to move your career ahead. This means putting into play high-probability strategies to optimize your chances for a successful career.

As the bodybuilder's core develops, she also works to build her other muscle groups for a complete system. This complete system provides the edge to compete well and win. Winning builds a trusted reputation of performance and creates additional opportunities to compete.

Consider the type of talent evaluation and placement process at work in companies like GE. If talent is rolled up according to the recognition of work performed and potential, then leaders and human resource managers must have some insight into your level of performance. How do you differentiate yourself? By consistently contributing at a high level of excellence *and* making others aware of your influence on the results.

Leaders can't talk about what they don't know about. Naturally, they form perceptions about you based on their knowledge of you. These facts and perceptions come to the table in closed-door discussions about talent. They influence decisions on who will be highlighted as the talent rollups take place. Professionals with *known* influence (often based on their level of excellence in getting the job done) can FuelForward.

Engaging the FuelForward Accelerators means knowing how talent advancement works in your organization. You have to understand the rules of engagement to be in the game.

Consider This:

- How does talent advancement really work in your organization?

- Talk with knowledgeable people to understand the formal and informal processes that take place.

- How is the process different from what you expected?

- What might you need to focus on more: Building Your Foundation, or Engaging Accelerators?

You can be sure both formal and informal processes take place in every organization. Behind the scenes of informal processes are discussions about the perceived capabilities and character of employees. You can leverage your expert execution by influencing opportunities to be discussed—and by influencing what's said about you in those discussions.

Your FuelForward Accelerators for getting promoted include forming a positive Reputation, gaining broad Reach to become known as a capable contributor to the business, and building credible professional Relationships. These three Accelerators have the greatest effect on your career progression—significantly greater than your execution alone. That means unless you're proactively working on little

known yet highly influential strategies that allow you to
FuelForward, your progress is likely to take longer.

In my interviews, successful mid-level and senior-level
executives shared insights from their personal experiences
on how execution alone won't move the needle. Ralph de
Chabert is the Chief Diversity Officer for Brown-Forman
Corporation. Here's what experience has taught him:

> You have to be managing the environment in order to
> get opportunities for increased visibility. So, you can
> be doing your job, head down, doing a wonderful job.
> But if you're really going to move up either within the
> function or within the organization as a whole, you
> have to be seen as someone who the person above
> you and the person above them says, "This person is
> really pretty good. We've seen him doing certain
> things and we feel good about him. Therefore, we
> think we should be advocating for him." So, you've got
> to manage the environment to get people in the talent
> reviews to have positive discussions about you.

Realize that to advance, the critically important
performance "punch list" is only one factor. It's even more
critical to have the FuelForward Accelerators in your toolkit.
Ralph added these insights on managing your career in what
people call "playing the game":

> Playing the game is not all bad. Losing yourself in the
> game is terrible. There's a big difference. But once you
> understand that politics is not this ugly thing and that
> successful people manage their environments very
> well, then you figure out where you want to play, at

what level you want to play, and not deceive yourself in the process. Be clear about how to be true to yourself while recognizing that people need to know you. They just do.

Don't sit and wait for the human resources process to move you along in your career. You can and must help it along. Strategies in this book teach you how to do just that.

●   ●   ●

REMEMBER:

⇒ Talent assessments and decisions are being made, whether you realize it or not.

⇒ Two fundamental principles will drive career progression:
   1. Building Your Foundation
   2. Engaging Accelerators

⇒ The most important first step in your career is having a strong Foundation of knowledge and skills to do the job. This foundation is comprised of your *Expertise*, *Experiences*, and *Execution*.

⇒ Your Career FuelForward Accelerators are:
   • Forming a positive *Reputation*
   • Gaining broad *Reach* to become known as a capable contributor to the business

- Building credible professional *Relationships*.

These accelerators have the greatest effect on your career progression, significantly greater than your execution alone.

Resource:

How do you rate on using these practices to accelerate your career? Go to *www.FuelForwardBook.com/resources* to take the FuelForward Career Practices Assessment.

Chapter Four

Own It

Yes, I think the scales are tipping toward personal accountability versus "my leader is accountable for my advancement." People have a perception that leaders spend a big percentage of their time, 20 to 80 percent, leading the team, watching out for my development, planning my next role.

That's not true. They've got their hands-on work making things happen. They're not only in a position leading people. They're leading their own initiatives. So, one of my jobs is to make sure my leader knows what I'm interested in, what I want to learn, where I aspire to go next—or what I don't want to do.

My personal accountability is to network myself, go out and ask questions. I make relationships with people who are part of the organization, so I can find out what it's like in other areas. My leader is not going to find out what that's like and report it to me. I have to do that on my own.

–Jeff Nally, Executive Coach and Coaching Practice Leader

Consider This:
You own your career. In what ways are you proactively managing your future?

My Career Ladder is Waiting

You may have entered your career with the preconceived notion that a ladder with your name on it awaits your arrival. All you do is step on the first rung and get started on your way to the top. You simply have to work hard.

Yes, absolutely do a great job in your work. That's a fundamental requirement for getting opportunities to advance. But wake up. It may get you a nice pat on the back, but as mentioned earlier, hard work alone won't automatically get you the next promotion.

As reality sets in, you realize these ladders don't even exist. Even though a company may have defined career paths for certain functions, they, too, are not absolute. You don't automatically move up because it's your turn, or because you've paid your dues, or because your performance is great.

Don't look to the human resources department for making sure you get promoted. Professionals in human resources understand the skills and competencies needed for the organization to reach its strategic goals. They either acquire or help develop that talent and move it, like a chess piece, into position for strategic gain. *You* have a lot to do with whether or not you'll be on the chessboard.

Although there's not a career ladder with your name on it, there is a watch list of high-potential employees who may be considered for promotions. This list changes as potential talent moves on and off it. (Review Chapter Three: *The FuelForward Model for Career Success* for more about this point.)

The Buck Stops with You

Remember, no one else is responsible for your opportunities. There's no entitlement. The company doesn't owe you a promotion. It's up to you to ensure your leaders know you are ready for added responsibility. You're accountable.

Nancy Torra, a project manager for a Fortune 100 healthcare and well-being company, has this advice about accountability:

> Career management is 100 percent your responsibility. In the ideal world, you would have somebody looking at people's performance and personality and saying, "You would be great at X job." But that doesn't happen. So it's all about your proactively working on your career and not waiting for it to happen.

To be accountable for managing your career means that in addition to constantly stellar execution, you're learning about different departments and roles in the company. You're evaluating your goals and aspirations, assessing your progress, and actively engaging the FuelForward Accelerators that will help you move ahead.

Nancy Torra shared another strategy she uses in managing her career:

> I have been able to get to know people from different areas—not only to help me find a role or get to an interview, but to tell me more about a position, to

explain what they do and what the role means. I connect with other people within the organization, so I can determine whether another job is something I want to do. That has been helpful for me.

While career management is a shared responsibility with the company, and processes such as performance reviews, mapping your career, and mentoring programs support career management from the company's standpoint, they don't replace the need to explore and chart your own career path—and take action to pursue it.

Accountability Drives Your Progress

Accountability, though not readily thought of as a career differentiator, is the power that makes your career journey come together. Remember, a career is a two-way commitment. You own building your skills and gaining the experiences necessary to be a strong contributor to the organization's goals. Your personal growth and contributions allow you to advance. As long as you live up to your side of the deal, the organization commits to wages, benefits, purposeful work, and potential opportunities for personal development and career advancement.

I remember being in GE when the GE African American Forum, GE Women's Network, and other affinity groups were emerging. Jack Welch and other leaders regarded them as self-help groups that sponsored training and mentoring, and they provided exposure opportunities for their members. It was up to the groups' leaders to determine and address members' needs. It was also up to the members to take advantage of the development the groups offered.

These types of groups still play an important role in many companies. Yet, they must ensure their offerings remain relevant as the needs of diverse professionals and their companies evolve.

Accountability is of special importance to women as they manage their careers. Why? One career accelerator noted earlier is the need for a network of influential acquaintances and sponsors. Women's networks tend to be less developed than men's in this area.

In fact, the scarcity of women in senior leadership roles often contributes to weaker networks. The upper ranks of leadership are sparsely populated by women, even though women make up nearly 50 percent of the workforce.[iv] Less than 5 percent of Fortune 500 CEOs are female.[v] Given these statistics, a woman's network of senior women who may help other women move up is smaller than the network men naturally have.

Own It

Some professionals feel that career management beyond focusing on day-to-day execution is too time-consuming. But strategies available throughout this book can help. Just like nurturing flowers, if you water them a little each day, the flowers will bloom beautifully.

The power of what you can achieve has the most to do with the power of your *personal accountability*. I can't stress that point enough.

Consider This:

Career Management Accountability Checklist

To be accountable for managing your career means that in addition to stellar execution every day, you are proactively thinking about and working on your career.

Use this checklist to help you focus on important areas of career management.

My Professional Goals and Aspirations
- What do I want to be when I grow up?
    - What types of responsibilities or roles would I like to move into over the course of my career?
- What skills and experiences do I need to acquire for my desired career path?
- What are the next two roles that would help me acquire those skills and experiences?
- Am I prepared for the next career step?
    - What strengths do I possess?
    - What skills do I need to develop?
- What are the perceptions about me across the organization?
    - Am I perceived as a star performer?
    - How do I influence those perceptions?
- Do I have acquaintances or working relationships with leaders across the organization?
- Am I benefiting from having a mentor?
- Am I leveraging and carefully managing opportunities that arise for making connections?

REMEMBER:

⇒ Only you are fully accountable for your career. There's no entitlement. You must take ownership and full accountability.

⇒ While career management is a responsibility the company shares with employees, they must chart their own career paths and take action to pursue them.

Resource:
Are you strategically planning ahead for your career path? Visit www.*FuelForwardBook.com/resources* to download a Career Planning worksheet.

Own It

48

Chapter Five

FuelForward Foundation: Execution

Capacity for Superior Execution

It is minutes before the Summer Olympics men's track relay race. The United States is up against Jamaica's record-setting medalists. The men on the U.S. team eagerly stretch and warm up for the start.

It's a huge race for the men on the U.S. team. Failure to nail the handoffs during the previous Olympic Games had cost them a medal-eligible finish. Dropping the baton during one of the handoffs created a four-year wait before they could try again.

They know the baton handoffs will be critical to their success this time. Preparation involved grueling hours of sweat-drenched conditioning and practicing handoffs over and over again. And now it's showtime. Anxious anticipation shows on their faces. The runners are set in their blocks. The gun goes off.

Each runner must complete 100 yards and pass the baton to the next runner with continued strong momentum. First handoff . . . successful! Second handoff . . . successful! Third handoff . . . nailed it!

The race reaches its fourth and final leg. An experienced U.S. athlete runs neck and neck with the favored Jamaican runner racing for the finish line. The crowd goes crazy.

The men run with every ounce of will and muscle they have inside. You can see the power in their legs and nearly breathless exertion on their faces with each stride. The Jamaican runner breaks over the finish line seconds before the U.S. runner. Jamaica wins the gold. The U.S. finishes with silver.

High Performance at Work, Too

Gold or silver medal, that's high performance! The athletes have done the hard work to be prepared. They had the skills required to execute at a level of excellence. All of that applies at work, too.

We tend to think of execution related to our jobs as simply coming to work every day, going to meetings, and checking off tasks on our to-do list. But in the context of moving your career forward, think of execution as both the "what" you do and "how high" you can perform—like the Olympic men's track relay team.

When you think of a high performance sports athlete or team, whom do you think of? What characteristics stand out in your mind to make them high performers?

I bet your list includes characteristics like "gives 100 percent every time," "stands out as far better than others," "always gets the job done," "plays to win," "has mental focus and toughness," "dependable," "statistics say it all," and "best average in the league."

Consider the coaches who put together these high performance teams, recruiting the best athletes and mix of talent possible. For example, NCAA Division I Basketball coaches are heavily recruiting the McDonald's All Americans, Mr. Basketballs, the top scorers, and the top center rebounders. Their goal is to stack the deck with the best skill and track record of execution they can get. It dramatically increases their odds of forming a winning team.

Execution in your career is the same way. Leaders are looking for talent who "gives 100 percent every time," can "always get the job done," "plays to win," "has the mental focus and toughness," is "dependable," has "statistics that say it all," and "knows how to hit the numbers."

Setting High Performance Standards

When it comes to evaluating execution, five primary high performance standards represent the characteristics leaders look for when they promote or hire employees:

- Problem Solver
- Accountable
- Consistently Exceeds Expectations
- Gets Things Done
- Customer-focused

Let's take a closer look at each of these important characteristics.

Problem Solver

Are you proactive in solving problems, or do you tend to point out problems and whine about them? If you're a good problem solver, you:

- Proactively identify potential problems.
- Proactively assess and mitigate potential risks.
- Seek and face challenges head-on instead of assuming or wishing problems will go away.
- Take responsibility for finding solutions to problems.

51

- When a problem arises, understand it and determine potential solutions before taking it to your leader.
- Create solutions that establish systems to implement permanent solutions, not just Band-Aids.

Accountable

Do you take full accountability for your areas of responsibility, good or bad? If you are accountable, you:

- Deliver on commitments, consistently meeting or exceeding them.
- Come through every time. You're dependable. You have a strong track record of doing what you say you will do.
- Proactively communicate if a potential delay arises.
- Don't become a victim of challenges but take responsibility for finding solutions to them.
- Don't let excuses handicap your willingness to take action.

Consistently Exceeds Expectations

Do you consistently go above and beyond what's expected of you? Make sure you:

- Have a clear understanding of what actions are expected from you. Eliminate ambiguity.
- Plan your work and work your plan.
- Don't just meet your numbers or goals but give an all-out effort to beat the numbers.

Gets Things Done

Are you the go-to person who the organization can count on to get things done? If you're known to deliver, you:

- Work smart on the right things versus wasting critical effort on less important tasks.
- Can delve into the weeds, knowing how to get the right details to make decisions; but, you can get out of the weeds to make quick, strategic decisions.
- Identify and access the resources you need to complete every job.

Customer-focused

Are you an advocate for your customers, ensuring there's an outside-in, reality-based perspective driving priorities and decisions? The best customer-focused organizations are attentive to:

- *External customers.* Realize the significance of external customers on driving business priorities and outcomes.
- *Internal customers.* Realize the relationship of internal departments on the company's ability to serve customers well. Ensure internal customers are served well.
- *Delivering optimal service levels.* Provide exceptional standards of quality in terms of service to customers and product performance.
- *Partnering for customer success.* Partner with customers to understand their needs and find solutions that enable their success. Help the business become a value-add partner that customers seek out first to help them.

Consider This:

How would you rate yourself on these five high performance standards? Use a scale of 1 to 5, with 1 for "I really need to work on that" and 5 for "I do pretty well on this one."

Problem Solver	1	2	3	4	5
Accountable	1	2	3	4	5
Consistently Exceeds Expectations	1	2	3	4	5
Gets Things Done	1	2	3	4	5
Customer-focused	1	2	3	4	5

Early in her career as an account executive, Tracey Purifoy-Moneypenny, a director at a higher education institution, began demonstrating these standards of high performance. Here's how these standards have carried over to other roles in her career:

> I'm always thinking long term, past the immediate decision and what those implications might be. I'm not just thinking for right here, right now. Rather, I'm always thinking two or three steps ahead, because that's the way I am.
>
> My title aside, we are all in this together. I don't think of it as them or us. It's us together. I ask for feedback on decisions. "Okay, how do we counter this? How do we incorporate this?" So, I'm brainstorming all the time about how to improve our processes or what

we can do to make sure this doesn't happen again if something falls through the cracks. We are constantly asking, "What can we do better? How can we make this easier or more efficient?"

Tracey's attitude, problem-solving ability, and consistent level of execution have been recognized. Leaders request her input on decisions, and she's often asked to share her best practices.

Why is This High Level of Execution Important?

Organizations are challenged every day to meet their business goals as well as the demands of their customers. If they don't meet these goals and expectations, the consequences can be brutal. Wall Street doesn't care why the company may have failed to meet its financial projections. The pure fact of failure causes a ripple effect. Sales declines cause a tightening of the belt and lost market share. Workers lose their jobs. The stock price takes a hit.

Companies large or small, public or private are held to the same performance expectations of working hard every day to meet goals and fulfill missions. What company do you know that has a goal of decreasing sales and profitability? That sounds ridiculous, doesn't it? Goals and expectations are set for growth and for moving forward, not backward. Therefore, companies have to be innovative and aggressive in attaining their goals if they want to remain competitive and grow. When they fail to achieve performance at levels that drive growth, sales decline and profitability shrinks. Their efforts shift to significantly reducing costs to survive.

Unfortunately, we can find clear examples of declining company performance and the resulting demise or near failure of these businesses: **Kodak, Hostess, Hewlett-Packard,** and **Groupon.** They are icons in our country's history or new, promising ventures on the horizon. It hurts everyone when their failure to innovate causes their decline. It's not any one person's fault. Of course, leadership's vision, direction, and investment decisions steer the ship. But the ability to execute brings the vision to life.

Kodak was the market leader in film manufacturing and photo processing. Kodak was synonymous with film, like Kleenex is with tissues. Kodak failed to see the future and did not invest in innovations with new technologies. Company leaders discounted the wave of new, non-traditional competition. As a result, they were forced to sell much of their intellectual property to generate cash and stay afloat.

Hewlett-Packard fell into a similar situation with lack of innovation and competitive awareness. The company experienced turmoil and churn at the CEO level, which created instability and lagging performance.

While challenged with high labor costs, **Hostess** also failed to keep up with emerging health trends. Consumer preferences were shifting to lower fat options and to newer varieties of snacks from competitors. Price competition within the snack categories made the Hostess cost position a liability. Hostess failed to execute in a new competitive environment. The company was liquidated, and the brand was purchased by private equity.

Groupon depended on its go-to-market strategy longer than it should have, tiring consumers by filling their inboxes with push offers they didn't want. Their sales and stock price declined dramatically. Groupon has been able to execute a turnaround strategy, however, with innovations using pull marketing strategies. Will they be able to reinvent themselves as market demands change?

Dangerous Trap

These companies were successful for a long time. Even as they were in decline, cash carried them for a while and people continued to feel secure. In this type of situation with companies comfortably riding along, an employee attitude of entitlement can set in—entitlement to hold the job, receive a paycheck, and come to work every day because of their years of loyalty to the company. This is a dangerous trap to fall in. Eventually, the company's inability to choose the right direction and its inability to execute catch up with it.

With so much on the line, companies are looking for solid employees and leaders they can count on to get the job done. You can count on them. You know what you're going to get. You can just about bet on the outcome. Bottom line—that's what matters.

These employees are committed to their work and committed to a standard of excellence. They take personal responsibility for developing the skills and gaining the experience they need to do outstanding work and add value. High performers have an outcomes-based mindset. They are motivated by the drive to deliver.

The members of the men's Olympic track relay teams had to commit to developing the skills necessary to first make the team. Then they had to get prepared to give their best for each qualifying race and the final medal run. Likewise, successful companies need employees who show up to contribute at their highest level of potential.

Build a Strong Foundation for Solid Execution: Expertise and Experiences

You own the resolve to advance your skills and gain the experiences necessary to be a strong contributor to the company's goals. Professionals who have been in the workforce for some time have developed a level of expertise in their technical areas. That makes it easy to become complacent and go along doing your job every day. But as fast as technology and customer needs are changing, you have to continually learn and grow. Your company is constantly evaluating the A, B, and C talent and determining its talent needs. An organization is only as good as its weakest link. Weak links don't survive long.

Companies will often invest in developing the skills and competencies of their employees. This may come in the form of training, different roles and responsibilities, or even working on projects. Take these opportunities seriously. Learn all that you can. Ask questions. Understand the fundamentals of how the business operates and how your department and role contribute to outcomes for the business. Seek opportunities to develop your professional skills in each position to enhance your value and effectiveness.

I know you can't imagine fitting one more thing into your day. But look at your personal development as one of your most important priorities. How can you contribute at your best if you don't have the skills or knowledge from past experiences to solve current challenges?

With today's e-Learning technology so readily accessible, most companies offer continuing education online at no cost to employees. Explore the catalog to determine which online courses can benefit you most. Many companies also provide tuition reimbursement for continuing education through colleges and universities. Earning an advanced degree may make a difference.

In addition, you may be a member of a professional association. Many of these associations offer ongoing programs. Some with certification programs provide continuing education credits. Consider earning new certifications that will enhance your skill set.

Nancy Torra, project manager for a Fortune 100 healthcare and well-being company, shared her perspectives on building a foundation for execution:

> You have to differentiate yourself. I feel having a master's degree speaks volumes. It says you're willing to go to the next level and learn more, and bring the knowledge to the workplace. A lot of people believed in me more *after* they saw I had an MBA and knew I went after a higher degree level.
>
> You can differentiate yourself by trying to improve yourself, maybe looking at soft skills or technical skills you can learn. My employer offers a lot of free technical skills training online. I take advantage of the different workshops offered.
>
> Also, bring your "A" game to work and always try to learn as much as possible. You may need that at the next level. A desire to learn is an influencer; people see that. It's about going to the position and proving you can do it.
>
> Still, you have to come to work every day and concentrate on what you're doing, not so much on

your next move. But that's important, so keep an eye on it.

Building a strong foundation for solid execution is your responsibility. Where do you begin? By focusing on these questions:

- What are the company's priorities?
- Where is the industry or your technical area trending?
- How are the needs of customers and the marketplace changing?
- What development areas were identified in your performance review or 360° feedback?
- Which of the five high performance standards— problem solver, accountable, consistently exceeds expectations, gets things done, or customer-focused— could use development?
- What experiences in your current role and along your career path will help you prepare to give your best?

Get Feedback to Uncover Best Areas for Development

Performance feedback is an important source for determining where to focus your personal development. You owe it to yourself to pursue getting honest feedback that will help you grow. However, some managers have a hard time delivering that honest feedback.

I've heard from many leaders and human resource managers that their company's culture is "nice." Managers are afraid to give their employees the direct, tough feedback they need to hear. Employees take the word of their managers, believing their boss's direction is the pathway to the personal development that will help them progress. Your manager holds considerable power in pointing you in a direction where you believe your efforts should be focused.

However, in a "nice" culture, professionals find the feedback they receive is often surface-level and generalized. Giving feedback becomes a formality so the manager can check the box and say, "That's done!"

Giving direct feedback is one of the toughest parts of a manager's job and causes a great deal of stress. People don't like conflict. It's uncomfortable. Managers don't realize that stress increases when the lack of openness and honesty keeps the real issues from being dealt with. They also don't realize that poor feedback inhibits the full potential not only of the individual but also the organization.

How do you navigate a situation like that? First, honest discussions are tougher when a relationship is tense or hardly exists. You can't simply wait until you want direct feedback and then abruptly ask a manager to be honest with you. How difficult would it be for you?

Even if you think your manager doesn't care about you, take the initiative to forge connections with her anyway. Say hello every day. Share something that happened. Inquire about her weekend. Be curious about how an important meeting went for her. Ask what you can do to help when she's working on a big project.

You also want to schedule time to meet with your manager on an ongoing basis. These can be periodic update meetings in which you share what you're working on and your accomplishments. Don't just ask for a meeting when you have a problem to bring up, or she will dread it when she sees you coming. Instead, make each conversation an open, ongoing dialogue.

Eric, a general manager of a manufacturing company, learned early in his career the value of making connections with his boss. When he was a purchasing assistant, he set up a standing meeting with his boss every two weeks. Eric would begin the meeting with updates on accomplishments and activities completed. Then he would share updates on projects in progress and make note of areas where he may need his boss's help. Lastly, he would ask if his boss needed his help on anything at the time. These regular connections developed his boss's knowledge of his contributions and enhanced his boss's perception of him as an important team member.

When asking for feedback, request examples of specific behaviors your boss observed in specific situations and especially what you've done well. That way, you can pinpoint a successful action, interaction, or approach. Use the feedback to learn where you can improve.

Consider This:
• Ask what you can do today to make performance discussions with your manager more meaningful.
• Connect and engage on a more personal level with your boss by asking about outside interests.
• Keep your boss updated on the projects you're working on.
• Ask for specifics and be willing to improve.

Feedback from Many Sources

Feedback can come from a variety of sources. You can ask your manager but also your mentors, peers, former managers, and even customers or suppliers. Take advantage of getting feedback from a diverse set of individuals. A 360° review is a good tool to get objective feedback from a variety of people and groups.

Sharon is a mid-level program manager for a mid-sized multinational company. Her role requires interacting with individuals and teams in a variety of departments across the company. A 360° review is not a standard part of the annual review process for those below senior level in the company. So Sharon worked with her human resources manager to arrange getting feedback from this confidential and information-rich process.

Specifically, Sharon sought feedback from her manager, peers, leaders, and team members in other departments. She learned about people's experiences working with her and their perceptions of how she demonstrated values of importance to the business. Sharon used that feedback to enhance the development plan that she and her boss had agreed upon following her annual performance review.

In small companies, close collaboration is often required on a day-to-day basis. However, don't make the mistake of assuming your manager or the owner is tuned in to your individual contributions. As in large organizations, these leaders are often focused on customers or putting out fires.

Instead, make it a point to schedule times to periodically share your work. Take time to ask for feedback on your technical skills, interpersonal skills, and other competencies important to your business. By using these insights to see opportunities, you can develop into an even more effective team member.

Execution Optimized—in Football and Business

Let's return to a sports analogy for a different perspective on what optimal execution looks like.

Imagine your favorite football team is leading its opponents 36–7 at halftime in a performance that was well beyond expectations. That's what happened early in a recent college football season during the University of Louisville and University of North Carolina football game at Cardinal Stadium.

Have you ever heard the saying, "Never give up?" Well, North Carolina came out in the second half and, little by little, clawed its way back into contention. The team scored an unbelievable 27 points in the second half. At the end of the fourth quarter, the game was a nail-biter.

What happened to Louisville's commanding lead? Did the players take their eyes off the goal? Did they get too comfortable and stop playing as a team? Have you ever been in that kind of situation when you started strong and suddenly your performance slipped?

With four minutes left in the game, the score was 34–39 with Louisville in the lead. But North Carolina had the ball with nine yards to the goal. Luckily for Louisville, North Carolina did not execute well at this critical point.

To be specific, the North Carolina receiver dropped the ball. The next play advanced the team to the three-yard line, followed by a false start. Then, the next play brought the team to fourth down with short yardage to the goal and only 1:49 minutes left to play. North Carolina's quarterback made a pass into the end zone, but the receiver dropped the ball with Louisville's defensive players all over him. One minute remained, and Louisville regained possession of the ball, winning by the skin of its teeth.

During his post-game interview, Louisville's coach made a statement that captures what often happens with failed performance in the workplace. "We didn't play all the way through. We didn't finish the game."

Let's contrast the University of Louisville's early season performance with its conference title clincher against Rutgers at the end of the season.

Louisville was down 14–3 at halftime. According to the report in the *Courier Journal*:

> The University of Louisville quarterback's performance with a broken wrist and sprained ankle was the most obvious display of toughness during Thursday night's 20–17 victory over Rutgers. But, the Cardinals don't win a share of their second straight Big East title, don't position themselves to make their first BCS bowl in six years, and definitely don't rally from an 11-point deficit on the road without that toughness throughout the roster.[vi]

Offensive lineman Alex Kupper said the Cards take their cue from quarterback Teddy Bridgewater. "He's just an unbelievable player, the way he fights," Kupper said. "When you're playing next to him, if you do anything less, it's shame on you. You have to fight *with* him." It wasn't only physical pains the Cards had to overcome. They had to show mental toughness, too.

What was the team's reward for this level of execution? An invitation to college football's esteemed BCS Sugar Bowl, where Louisville's performance was even hotter. The

Louisville Cardinals, nationally ranked at #23, were matched against the #4 team, University of Florida Gators. The Gators had beaten many opponents during the regular season. The Louisville Cardinals, the 14-point underdog, dominated the Florida Gators by a score of 33–23.

Let's translate this football example into the corporate environment. Obstacles are the challenges you face. What you do with those obstacles defines you. As you strive for accomplishment, dealing with obstacles makes the effort seem hard. But don't let them become excuses. Execution at its best means giving all you've got to reach the goal— nothing less.

A poor attitude toward overcoming challenges can damage a person's career. Companies need employees who take full responsibility to lead through the challenges that arise—people who commit to doing everything possible to succeed. A person who complains about situations or blames others for problems detracts from the progressive, performance-based culture leaders strive to create.

Leaders build teams with professionals who have a proven track record of solid execution and a positive, get-it-done attitude. The University of Louisville's football team demonstrated how!

Performance Execution: Your "A" Game is Required

Every leader I interviewed emphasized that your ability to execute is the foundation of your career and the other variables that allow you to compete. You can't even get on the career ladder without a level of performance execution that's recognized as significant by the organization.

A minimum set of performance criteria is defined for your role or by your manager. Often, these performance criteria are reestablished during the performance review process. Along with the goals for your department, they define your minimum performance expectations. Your boss and leaders compare your actual performance to this minimum expectation level as a way to determine your grade.

Performance execution is often characterized as A, B, or C level. A-level players are the "well above minimum expectations" performers. They earn the greatest right to play in the career game.

B-level players are seen as having promise. Companies often invest in them to develop their skills, giving them an opportunity to reach their A-level potential.

C-level players and below usually find themselves stuck in their career. Sometimes they leave the company, willingly or not. Why would leaders want C-level players on their team? What could they possibly get done with a group of C players?

Even if your company doesn't use the ABC grading system, leaders still evaluate employees in this way. It's a thought process, a grading system most leaders in U.S. companies grew up with in school. It's a way of ranking the employees on their teams so everyone generally understands.

Consider This:

What grade would leaders give you as they evaluate your performance execution? A? B? C? Or worse?

Sometimes, the ability to execute well can be a matter of job fit. Are you positioned in the role that best fits your skills, interests, and potential? While interviewing Rita Barksdale, a GE Healthcare executive, our discussion turned to how leaders regard performance in terms of job fit. She said:

> Performance is key. Fundamentally, you must have a track record for doing a good job to earn a second chance. In one incident, for example, I was approached about a leader who was significantly underperforming in his current role. I had to give an opinion of whether he was still right for our team.
>
> I reviewed his previous performance evaluations. Then, I talked with my management team and their peers to better understand the situation. The key question was this: Was he was simply in the wrong role or missing important success factors? We had to weigh all of that.

Remember the point made earlier about why the ability to execute is so important? Companies need to be able to compete in today's fierce global marketplace. Customers have many choices at their fingertips. If companies can't execute quickly and effectively, they'll lose business.

Managers don't have time to babysit employees on their team. They shouldn't have to. Professionals who want to succeed will step up. Those who go above and beyond to help their department meet its goals are the A players who will get the opportunities to advance.

A word of caution: Don't be so eager to get a promotion that you're always asking about the next opportunity. Just "doing your time" in a role doesn't mean you've gained the experience or demonstrated the skills needed to move on.

Remember, you need to make sure you're more focused on meeting the commitments of your current role than you are about making it to the next job. If you don't perform now, you simply won't have an opportunity to get promoted.

Making Personal Connections

Everything you do has to connect to achieving the mission, vision, and goals of the business and, to that end, to those of your customers, whether internal or external. The mission and vision are the company's true north that should guide its decisions. Be sure you know how *your* role connects to the mission, vision, and goals of the company and your department's needs.

If you don't know, make it a top priority to work with your manager to understand. Otherwise, what you work on, prioritize, or focus on will be disconnected. You'll fail to be known as a top performer, because you're not connected to what's important to the business. It is only when you make and act on this connection that you can have a real, recognizable effect within your sphere of influence—and be known as an A performer.

For example, if you're an accounting clerk, ensuring billing is accurate and receivables are processed in a timely manner affects the bottom line. Or you might be an engineer working on a small component that installs into a subsystem of a final product. Making sure the component's reliability supports the subsystem is critical to preventing product failures and, therefore, pleasing customers.

Being connected to company results is easier to see when you have a direct profit-and-loss or sales role. But they can still be defined for every role in the organization. Otherwise, your role wouldn't exist. Your manager or a mentor can be an excellent resource to help you define those connections clearly for yourself.

Execution in Your Organization

What does career-advancing star performance mean inside *your* company? Your department may have a defined set of competencies and values that can provide guidance for meeting and exceeding performance expectations. Consider developing your skills across the continuum—from novice to expert—and demonstrating your competence at each level.

So you won't stay in the lower levels very long, you need to demonstrate you're a fast learner, able to quickly and easily integrate these skills into your leadership style. In addition to the specific goals you and your manager develop during your performance review and career-planning conversations, your performance will be assessed on these core competencies. Make sure you know the expected competencies, values, and performance levels.

Everyone has an innate desire to do good work. Find that fire within yourself to become that star performer.

Consider This:
What does career-advancing star performance mean inside your company? What competencies and skills are required?

Executive Perspectives on Performance Execution

When it comes to performance execution, notice these quotes from interviews in *The Wall Street Journal* article, "How Women Can Get Ahead: Advice from Female CEOs." They provide practical guidance for understanding what it takes to succeed.

As mentioned earlier, Jack Welch, former CEO of General Electric, said: *"To get ahead, focus laser-like on performance... raise your hand for line jobs and tough, risky assignments. And, take advantage of rigorous performance reviews, which are the best time to get coaching and address concerns about bias."*

Angela Braly, former CEO of WellPoint: *"Be open to opportunity and take risks. In fact, take the worst, the messiest, the most challenging assignment you can find, and then take control."*

Beth Mooney, CEO of KeyCorp: *"I have stepped up to many 'ugly' assignments that others didn't want."*

Ellen Kullman, CEO of DuPont: *"As for the sanctity of performance, it drove my career: 'Accountability, performance, and external benchmarking.'"*

Heather Bresch, CEO of Mylan: *"I have a strong work ethic and was willing to do whatever it took to get the job done. There is simply no substitute for hard work when it comes to achieving success."*

Maggie Wilderotter, CEO of Frontier Communications: *"I don't disagree with Jack Welch that performance is the ticket to the dance. Unless you're delivering value, there is no right to move forward. I do disagree that all is fair in the workplace."*

In summary, these leaders are saying you have to position yourself in a role of influence to prove your performance and get ahead. A role of influence can be accomplished in two ways. The first approach is to use whatever role you're in to add tangible value within your sphere of influence. No matter what your role, you can position yourself to have influence. The second approach is to take a sales or profit-and-loss role that makes you directly accountable for business revenue or profitability metrics. Regardless of which approach you choose, connect your work to the important performance outcomes of the business and knock the ball out of the park.

●   ●   ●

REMEMBER:

⇒ Leaders look for the following characteristics when they promote or hire employees:
- Problem Solver
- Accountable
- Consistently Exceeds Expectations
- Gets Things Done
- Customer-focused

⇒ You are responsible for expanding your skills and gaining the experience necessary to be a strong contributor to the company's goals.

⇒ Your goal is to be an A-level player and become known as one.

⇒ Communicate with your boss. Be proactive in sharing updates on your work and accomplishments.

⇒ Ask for honest, direct feedback so you know where you stand. Be open-minded. Let what you learn help you improve.

⇒ Focus on executing well in your current job. Don't let working on your career distract you from being an A-level player.

⇒ Learn the formal and unwritten rules of talent management in your organization.

Engaging FuelForward Accelerators
Career FuelForward Model

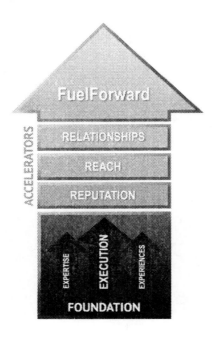

The Career FuelForward Accelerators—forming a positive *Reputation*, gaining broad *Reach* to become known as a capable contributor to the business, and building credible professional *Relationships*—have the greatest effect on your career progression. When built on a solid foundation of *Execution*, these accelerators are the most significant factors in moving your career forward. If you want to get promoted, *you have to strategically engage these FuelForward Accelerators.*

Chapters Six, Seven, and Eight introduce you to each of these practices in detail and provide strategies to apply them successfully.

Chapter Six

FuelForward Accelerator: Reputation

Perception is Reality

Jennifer, a vice president in a consumer products company, had a conversation with Dave, the information technology director. The subject? Kevin, one of Dave's team members who had worked on a project with Jennifer's team.

Jennifer had a definite opinion about Kevin from the work he did with her team. She believed he was ineffective in bringing the solutions her department needed to streamline some of its critical processes. Dave hadn't observed this directly when working with Kevin, and no other problems with clients had come up. He wondered if Jennifer's perception was coming from her direct experience or from other members of her team. However, she was so convinced about Kevin's inability to support her team, she would accept nothing less than having someone else assigned to her department.

What happened to create Jennifer's perceptions about Kevin's abilities? Kevin's reputation could become a challenge as he attempts to move up in his career.

Your reputation is vital to gaining momentum in your career, whether inside or outside your current organization. The information others have about you is the basis for their perceptions. If they know little about you, your image may be heavily influenced by what one or two people have to say. If you don't attempt to recover from situations that have not gone well, they could potentially derail your career.

Proactively building your personal brand in a way that positively affects your career is mandatory, not optional.

How Does the Concept of Branding Translate to Individuals?

One year, I was watching the final segment of the Miss Universe pageant on television. In this contest, beautiful and talented young women from around the world compete for the title of Miss Universe. As they announced the winner, I was a little surprised. Some might argue that she wasn't the most beautiful among the contestants, but she certainly appeared to be talented and highly polished.

The comments I heard about her after the contest convinced me she was the right pick. Here's why: She came well prepared for each of the areas she was judged in. Not only the judges but also the other women she competed against admired her. She used the traits of a powerful personal brand to demonstrate her character and build genuine relationships. These factors increased her chances of winning.

This chapter explains how you can apply these traits in the workplace to fuel your career forward.

What is Your Personal Brand?

Your personal brand is your *Reputation*—that is, your brand represents what people think about you. Fair or not, our innate tendency is to make a judgment about other people based on what we see and hear. We tend to take action and make decisions based on what we believe to be true.

Similarly, when you go to the store to buy groceries, electronics, appliances, or a car, you tend to favor certain brands. You make a purchase decision based on your belief in the brand's promise. Once you've used the product repeatedly, your choice becomes based on your experience with how the products lived up to their brand promise. What brands do you tend to buy most? What is it about the brand that makes you a loyal customer?

Purchasing decisions like these are worth millions of dollars to companies. They invest in communicating the brand's promise, in forming a brand image, and getting you to take a chance on its products based on the brand. You form a perception from its advertising, then your perception is confirmed or negated by your experience. Did the product live up to the brand's promise? Once the brand's reputation is formed, you base your ongoing purchase decisions on it.

Why Your Personal Brand Matters

The resulting effect of your brand on your career works the same way a product brand affects your purchase decision. Those who have the authority to choose who to place in different roles mainly have the Reputation of the potential candidates to go by. They weigh the track record of each candidate's brand reputation based on any objective or subjective information they have.

Where does this information come from? A combination of tangible results, personal interactions and observations, and views from others. People form ideas—whether right or wrong—about who you are, what you represent, your intelligence, your capacity to grow, and your abilities.

Perception is reality. The information others have readily available about you is used to form their perceptions. If there's little known about you, your image may be mostly influenced by hearsay.

Much of this inside information you may be unaware of because it's shared through informal conversations in the hallway, by the water cooler, or behind closed doors.

Advice from the Water-Cooler

Melanie Shook is the vice president of customer experience for Neustar, Inc., one of the world's top technology companies. As a leader, Melanie conveys firsthand how informal water cooler conversations actually work. She shared this advice:

> The types of things people talk about at the water cooler are mostly about a person's approach. How are you to work with as an individual? It's more about the "how" than the "what" you do. How are you doing things? How do people view you? How are you leading others?
>
> So it's really trying to get to who you are as a fundamental individual and how you contribute to the cause. That's a lot of the water-cooler conversation. You're just looking for fit, if you will. In the roundtable discussions, it's more about performance, results, and general characteristics about you.

This tells us your "water-cooler image" represents what people really think about you. Take the opportunity to shape information about you that's floating around. You own this, no one else.

Consider This:

- Are you aware of your "water-cooler image?" What are people saying about you in the informal conversations around the water cooler where they gather?
- Ask a trusted friend or mentor about people's perceptions of you. What are they hearing? Your boss is also a good resource for this type of feedback. Be open to what people share with you. Don't be defensive or try to explain. Listen and reflect.
- Based on what you learned, what do you feel good about? What do you think represents you well? What concerns you? What changes should you make as a result of these concerns?

Once your brand perception is established, it's pretty well set, and a negative image can be especially hard to change. Consider what a massive public relations effort it takes for a company to change any negative perceptions it might have.

For example, in the spring of 2010, more than 200 million gallons of oil spewed into the Gulf of Mexico. I recall the somber images of oil-soaked seagulls and dead fish lying on what used to be white-sand beaches. The livelihood of the Gulf's seafood and vacation industries was obliterated. It took weeks for the company responsible, British Petroleum (BP), to stop the oil leak, and now it's taking years for the

Gulf of Mexico to recover from the devastation. BP has spent millions of dollars on advertising its response to the crisis and its commitment to reversing the devastation. Overcoming its damaged reputation as a quality, environmentally responsible company will take a barrage of consistent messaging and actions for several years.

The same holds true for you as an individual managing your personal brand. If your image is sliding down a negative slope, it will take time and consistent effort to rebuild it. Even if you have a positive or indifferent brand image, any desire to change others' perceptions will take time and consistent effort.

The Value of a Brand

Brand matters because it establishes a certain value. For example, many people are willing to pay a premium for Apple products, because Apple has a track record of superior performance and extensive features. Apple promotes a brand promise that delivers time and time again. Before its current reputation was established, Apple had to earn the right to command a premium price and receive the respect it enjoys today.

The more a brand is perceived as valuable, the more the brand is worth, and the more attention it gets. People make buying decisions based on perceived value. Managers hire or promote based on perceived value.

Therefore, your goal isn't simply to build a surface-level image. Rather, it's to establish a brand that has a high perceived value, one that decision makers are willing to invest in. Those investments in professionals with high perceived value come in the form of exposure opportunities, mentors, sponsors, and maybe even promotions. A brand with a high perceived value has earned the trust that performance is there, that it has the potential to handle the future opportunities and challenges you may face.

Remember, branding is earned. People don't believe in your brand promise just because of what you say. Like trust, it takes work and time to build.

I interviewed a senior professional who had seen some professionals portray a highly competent and capable image, but beneath the surface, their capabilities were shallow. They seemed to advance because they knew the right people. In this case, after a senior leader had been promoted, he pulled other people he knew along with him.

However, for one of the professionals, the story did not end favorably. He could not follow through on his brand promise due to poor performance. He was forced to take a step back in his career.

It's human nature to go with the people you're most comfortable with. But if you're the leader pulling others up, do your homework. Or, if you're the employee being pulled, make sure you can fulfill your brand promise and realistically stretch to meet the expectations of the role.

Building a Credible, High-Value Personal Brand

What is the secret to building a credible, high-value personal brand? Putting three critical factors to work. These factors apply whether you're looking to advance within your current company or wish to expand your career to a different organization.

Three powerful brand traits have the greatest effect on your Reputation:

- Stand Out from the Crowd
- Well-known
- Perceived Runway

Brand Trait #1: Stand Out from the Crowd

You can't stand out if you blend in. If you're like everyone else around you, how will you get noticed? Professionals who stand out from the crowd are above average and clearly distinguish themselves in their track records of execution, their professionalism, and their executive presence.

Two elements comprise *Stand Out from the Crowd*:

- Strong Track Record of "What" and "How"
- Professionalism and Executive Presence

Strong Track Record of "What" and "How"

In terms of your performance track, your personal brand record is measured on the basis of the "what" and the "how"—that is, what you do or achieve, your ability to execute, and how you get things done.

Melanie Shook provided a sneak peek into what leaders look for when they discuss and make talent decisions. She said:

> What leaders look for falls into two primary areas. One is, "What are your core capabilities? What can you do?" So that's all of your functional skills, all the contributions, and the tangibles, if you will. And that's where we focus a lot.
>
> The other piece that I put a 50-percent focus on, and I've seen our company shift to that direction, is *how* you go about getting the results. So the first part

is all about results, performance, execution, and all of the tangibles. The second piece is what I call the value system, or the success factors, looking at how you go about getting results. Do you leave dead bodies along the way, but you get results? Or do you actually make things better as you get results? So I look at the "how" as well as the "what."

Then if you're a people leader, I have one more dimension: the leadership talent you bring to the table. How are you fostering an environment in which others can perform and grow? Are you leading that? Are you making others better within your organization?

What: The "what" represents your ability to deliver results. Do you achieve the performance objectives of the organization? How are your results measured?

Going back to our discussion on execution, your ability to execute above minimum expectation levels is foundational. The company needs to have solid performers and strong contributors to meet their goals. So your ability to execute is fundamentally why you have a job. Recall, too, that fulfilling your responsibilities in your current job is your first and most important concern.

When it comes to evaluating your "what"—your track record of performance execution—leaders look for five primary high performance standards:

- Problem Solver
- Accountable
- Consistently Exceeds Expectations
- Gets Things Done

- Customer-focused

Leaders want to see a track record in these areas that demonstrates your ability to deliver the results the business requires. (Refer to Chapter 5: *FuelForward Foundation: Execution* for details on each of these important characteristics.)

How: The "how" is your EQ, or emotional intelligence, and leadership—your positive influence on the people in the organization. "How" you work with others helps you develop either respected and trusted relationships, or disrespectful and untrustworthy relationships. Just as in your personal life, your work life revolves around relationships.

The brand perceptions related to your ability to execute are not one-dimensional. How you achieve results can be as important as what you achieve, especially as you move up in levels of greater responsibility and authority. No matter what your position or level in the organization, the way you work with others influences the effectiveness of those around you and the work environment itself.

Leaders promote professionals who have a positive, energizing influence on their teams. Attitudes, accountability, and the commitment level of employees largely affect employee engagement. Professionals with an engaging yet results-oriented image—a balance between the "what" and the "how"—usually achieve greater and more consistent results. This image portrays the type of leadership style most organizations want their leaders to embody.

These five primary traits characterize leaders with strong emotional intelligence (EQ):

- Values and Integrity
- Collaboration and Teamwork
- Respect for Others
- Engages Employees at All Levels
- Leads in All Roles

Values and Integrity

Values are the ethics that drive your behavior and are critically important within an organization. They drive the culture and behaviors of its leaders and employees. The value of integrity is often called upon in daily interactions and decisions. Leaders need to know their employees are trustworthy in all their dealings.

Characteristics of *Values and Integrity* that stand out in emotionally intelligent leaders are:

- They care about their character and care what others think about it. Character is a priority.
- A set of values consistently guides their actions. Their decisions, actions, and words are consistent with the values that drive their character. What others see on the outside genuinely matches their character on the inside.
- They can be counted on to do the right thing. Honest and trustworthy, they make the call that prioritizes the best interests of the organization, customers, and employees.

Collaboration and Teamwork

A positive work environment in which employees are collaborating as healthy teams to deliver on the company's business goals is one that's ripe for rich employee engagement. Rather than working in silos and only showing concern for their own priorities, departments work across boundaries for the betterment of the organization at large. Engaged employees are more likely to take ownership, creating a collaborative culture of innovation, productivity, quality, service, and focus on customers. Workplaces with engaged employees make the "Best Places to Work" lists. They show higher growth rates over time.

Characteristics of *Collaboration and Teamwork* that stand out in emotionally intelligent leaders are:

- They share and receive open, constructive feedback. They deliver objective feedback in a way that respects others. They listen objectively and take action on constructive feedback shared by others.
- They give and share credit. They neither take all the credit for success nor all the blame when things go wrong. Goals are rarely achieved alone, so they give credit where credit is due. They take responsibility when things don't go exactly as planned.
- They work well with teammates on projects and when solving problems. They seek input and ideas from all team members. Their attitudes and actions reflect personal accountability.

Respect for Others

To have respect for someone means to treat him or her with a sense of worth and honor. Your words and actions toward a person show a level of esteem, regardless of position or title. A respectful work environment fosters collaboration, teamwork, and engagement. Showing respect for others demonstrates that no matter what our differences, everyone has an important role to play.

Characteristics of *Respect for Others* that stand out in strong emotionally intelligent leaders are:

- They treat others according to the Golden Rule—the way they would want to be treated. Empathy helps them be more understanding of other's thoughts and needs.
- They speak respectfully to others. They carefully choose their words and expressions in all forms of communication.
- They value and listen to others' opinions and respect ideas from all team members. They are able to respect opinions different from their own as they seek to understand another person's perspective.

Engages Employees at All Levels

Companies stuck in the old ways of hierarchical control and politics are missing opportunities. Employees on the front lines and in the middle layers of the organization deal directly with customers and keep the operation running day in and day out. These employees know where the challenges and opportunities are. Good ideas often come from these layers of the organization. Employees who are asked to share ideas often solve problems. When they have opportunities to make meaningful contributions to the business, they tend to be more engaged, happier in their jobs, and retained at a higher rate.

Characteristics of *Engages Employees at All Levels* that stand out in emotionally intelligent leaders are:

- They welcome and invite ideas from everyone. Realizing they don't have all the answers, they're confident in asking others for their opinions and ideas.
- They give their teammates meaningful opportunities to contribute through their work.
- They help teammates connect to the mission and objectives of the organization. They keep their team members informed of company priorities, helping them understand the importance of their role to the organization.

Leads in All Roles

Every person within an organization can be a leader. You don't need a title to be accountable for achieving business results or to influence others in the organization.

Every day, you face many crossroads in the decisions you have to make. Employees who feel empowered in their roles have a greater sense of ownership in the company's success.

Characteristics of *Leads in All Roles* that stand out in emotionally intelligent leaders are:

- They take responsibility for what needs to be accomplished. Aware of what needs to be done, they willingly pitch in. They avoid saying, "It's not my job."
- They can see and communicate a vision for the end result and work with others to build a plan to get there. They visualize the end goal of a project and can engage others in determining how to accomplish it.
- They effectively influence others to act with and without authority. They build trust and respect with

others in the organization, engaging their peers and direct reports in accomplishing goals.

- They groom, grow, and develop people, mentoring others in the organization to develop technical, interpersonal, and leadership skills.

Your organization has probably identified values and competencies that provide additional guidance in these areas. Are you aware of them? Do you use them to assess where your efforts need attention?

Consider This:

How would you rate yourself on these five Emotional Intelligence traits? Use a scale of 1 to 5, with 1 for "I need to really work on that" and 5 for "I do pretty well on this one."

Values and Integrity	1	2	3	4	5
Collaboration and Teamwork	1	2	3	4	5
Respect for Others	1	2	3	4	5
Engages Employees at All Levels	1	2	3	4	5
Leads in All Roles	1	2	3	4	5

Professionalism and Executive Presence

Have you ever heard the saying, "First impressions are lasting?" Even before a word is said, people form perceptions based on what they see.

The second dimension of *Stand Out from the Crowd*, professionalism and executive presence, is not only demonstrated through what people see on the outside. It's also represented verbally and nonverbally: by what you say and don't say, your demeanor, and how you carry yourself.

All eyes are on you. Impressions are set from any and all of these attributes:

- *Dress:* for the job you want, neat and pressed
- *Attitude:* positive
- *Speech and Tone:* respectful
- *Demeanor:* collaborative
- *Engagement:* full and customer-centered

Your total package makes an impression. Your presence in how you engage with others also makes a huge impression. Given all of these dimensions, professionalism and executive presence are not necessarily black and white or one-size-fits-all. A person's values, experiences, and biases will influence the impressions they form about you.

Let's test this notion. As you read the following situations, what impressions come to mind?

- When you see a homeless person on the street, do you automatically have an impression of that person?
- When a man is slouching in his seat or yawning in a meeting or tapping his finger on the table, what impression do you have of him?
- When you're talking with a woman and she's silent on the other end of the phone, what impression do you have of her?
- When you're on a conference call and only one or two people are doing all the talking, what impression does that create?

When you pictured each of these situations in your mind, did you form immediate perceptions of the individuals described? Why?

Our human nature is to form perceptions based on what's in front of us. Therefore, be mindful of the impression you're creating and what your actions, words, and demeanor say about you. They are usually easy to control.

In our interview, Melanie Shook provided a leader's perspective on professionalism and executive presence. She said:

> Professionalism is a softer attribute that isn't quantitative but more qualitative about an individual. So you can't really measure and put a scale on how professional someone is, but you know some of the elements you're looking for. Could you put this person in front of a customer? Can he articulate his points? Does he visually add value? Or do you have to be concerned that he's going to come in looking a mess? All those softer elements may not be black and white, but they're important because you want to make sure they complement what you're trying to accomplish.
>
> I look at some elements like professionalism and I say, "I can't really teach someone that." That's a non-negotiable I expect you to come in the door with, versus elements I can help a person develop.

Your professionalism and executive presence reflect how mindful you are of the importance of these characteristics, and whether you even care about them. They show your ability to fit the character of what's expected at successive levels. That doesn't mean you will fit a certain stereotype. It means you'll be able to demonstrate respected leadership values and characteristics.

Professionalism and executive presence develop early on and, by paying attention, will continue to mature over the course of your career.

Dress

You've heard the saying, "If you want to advance, dress for the job you want, not the one you have."

That means dress according to your aspirations so others can picture you at the next level. Also, keep in mind that business casual dress is more "business" than "casual." Many people get too comfortable with casual days at work, and that can reflect badly.

Some companies have a higher dress standard for people in customer-facing roles. However, as you move into senior leadership roles, you have to be prepared for whatever you may face during your workday. You could end up in front of a customer or presenting at an important meeting that wasn't on your calendar when you arrived at work that day.

The tech industry is the anomaly to this reality. If you work for a tech company, the rules of engagement may be a little different in this area. Just make sure you're clearly aware of the written and unwritten standards in your organization.

Attitude

Your attitude and demeanor will send an impression without your saying a word. What kind of attitude do you bring? I once worked with a lady who was so negative that no one wanted to be around her. In meetings, she rarely had a positive comment to add. When coworkers suggested ideas, she'd say, "That won't work. We've tried that before."

Do you know anybody like that? Her only friends were the other negative employees that liked to commiserate about how much they hated the place. The solution? If you're having a bad day, leave it at the door. Nobody cares. Be known for your positive influence, not your negativity.

Speech and Tone

Jonathan was a project manager in the energy industry. His project involved team members from across the company. He was responsible for presenting updates at team meetings and leadership reviews.

As he entered the room for his first monthly leadership review, he dressed in one of his best suits and looked professional. But when he opened his mouth, the quality of his presentation did not match his appearance. He used terminology and acronyms the leaders weren't used to hearing. When some asked questions, Jonathan responded in a defensive tone.

What you say and how you say it are extremely important. Do you use proper grammar? Is your tone appropriate in both your verbal and written communications? Do you keep your composure? Or do you sometimes use inappropriate language? Does your body language contradict the words you're saying?

As you carefully prepare your communications and presentations, be aware of the effect you have on others.

Demeanor

Your demeanor is influenced by the values, motivations, and attitudes that drive your behavior. Know that your thoughts, feelings, and opinions on the inside come through on the outside.

Your demeanor includes your posture, the way you walk, your facial expressions and eye contact when communicating with others, and even how and what you say.

Your demeanor can change based on how you feel about a situation. It will come out in your body language and choice of words. Your demeanor can express whether or not you care about something, and even if you're engaged in what's going on around you.

Your demeanor is a powerful communicator. Be aware of what it's saying about you.

Engagement

How you engage also has an influence on perceptions of your professionalism and executive presence. Do you sit in positions of influence in meetings? Do you contribute to discussions with confidence? Do you actively listen and respect the values and opinions of others? Do you ask questions? Or are you just a body consuming space and oxygen in the room? If so, why even be there?

You were hired for your active, thoughtful, and engaged involvement in what needs to be accomplished. Even if you're an introvert, don't use that as an excuse to be silent.

Remember, perceptions are constantly being formed. Even more important, your voice, opinions, and ideas need to be heard. You could have the next great idea for the organization, but it may never have the opportunity to come to life.

Cultural norms influence how some people engage, so be sensitive to cultural differences and make an effort to include everyone. Also, be aware of the culture that influences the environment you're in, and be prepared to adapt to some degree. Even though you expect others to respect *your* culture, the organization itself has a culture that determines its own norms. So to be successful, become acutely aware of these norms and operate primarily within them.

People in the younger generations often believe they have a right to individuality and self-expression. But the truth is the organization gets to make the rules of its culture in terms of dress, values, behaviors, and overall image. In this regard, business tends to be conservative. Why? Because customers spend money with organizations they believe will live up to expected levels of performance, service, and quality.

Whatever your generation, you have a responsibility to adhere to the company's cultural values and norms. If you believe those don't fit your values and preferences, you can choose to find a better fit elsewhere. It serves neither you nor the company to stay when these do not align.

How do you add value to the organization through your engagement? Look in the mirror.

Brand Trait #2: Well-known

Professionals who are well-known have strong brand awareness. Let's test this theory.

If you were asked to make a list of brands, which ones would readily come to mind and why? You first think of those brands that have made a concerted effort to promote their name and what they stand for, right? You make purchase decisions based on brands you know and trust, correct?

Before promoting your personal brand, make sure you have a clear vision that guides your career. It will help you determine your brand.

Clear Vision: Building a well-known brand starts with having a clear vision of both what you want to do and what you want to be known for. Use this as a checklist to help you define a vision for yourself in these areas:

- What You Want to Do
  - Personal and Professional Goals
  - Purpose
  - Career Path
- What You Want to be Known For
  - Results and Effect on the Business
  - Expertise
  - Integrity and Values
  - EQ: Interpersonal Understanding and Influence
  - Organizational and Cultural Acumen

What You Want to Do

One leader I interviewed said most people think there's a career ladder figured out for you, just waiting for you to jump on. As discussed earlier, that's absolutely not true. It's up to you to seek information that helps you devise a career path and then share it with your manager and mentor. Make sure you're flexible and open to the fact that your path may change along the way.

Also, you don't necessarily have to define specific job titles on your career path. Rather, you can describe your aspirations by the type and scope of the job responsibilities you'd like to have. Your manager, human resources manager, or mentor can help you define the job titles as you build a path that's right for you.

When determining your career path, use a process that allows you to be thoughtful about important considerations. Begin with listing your personal and professional goals. This list of questions will help you do that.

- What are the most important priorities for me and my family in the next one, three, and five years?
- What do I feel is my life's purpose?
- What am I best at? Least effective at?
- What areas do I have potential to develop and grow into?
- What would I like to accomplish professionally in the next one, three, and five years?
- What tradeoffs might I need to consider, given my personal and family priorities and my strengths?
- What might my career path options be?
- What experiences and skills might I need in the next two to three steps on my career path?
- What roles will help me gain the experiences and skills I need along each step of my career path?
- What do I need to accomplish and learn, to grow and contribute fully in my current role?
- What are the key actions, milestones, and timeframes to help me reach my goals?

As you work through this career-planning process, talk with your family members or significant other to establish your goals and priorities. Careers are a family endeavor. It takes lots of support and sacrifice from these important people in your life to have a successful career.

Your manager, human resource manager, or mentor can help you pinpoint potential career paths and their required experiences and skills. Perhaps they can provide objective feedback about roles that may prove ideal for you. Also, talk to professionals in roles of interest to you. They can be a great resource of information and insight.

Some departments have career paths that guide certain functions. These are commonly found in areas such as IT, engineering, accounting, and finance. Of course, every career is different. But, guidelines help establish a progressive path for organizational development and assist in identifying what is required to advance.

What You Want to be Known For

When your name comes up during a conversation between leaders, what picture do you want them to have in mind about you? What brand perception do you want them to perceive? Kelly Schmidt, an IT director for Johnson & Johnson, shared some of the strategies she used to make others aware of what she wanted to be known for:

> I became known as a good technologist, able to manage business partners and so on. Then, I wanted to get experience in an area that took me away from managing people for a few years. People forgot about that aspect. So, I had to do my own little campaign to reorient people to my background.
>
> Within our company, it's common for people to change roles every two or three years. So, it's not unusual for people to have get-to-know-you

conversations with different people. "Hey, I've been in this role for two or three years. I'm beginning to think about my next career opportunity. I want you to know a little bit more about my background. Would you just keep me in mind for new openings?"

While doing that kind of networking campaign, rather than talk to people about what they already knew about me, I spent time talking about what they might have forgotten or what they hadn't seen recently. I subtly started to weave that into general conversations by using a tactic such as, "In my prior role managing people, this is what we had done." I talked about specific tactics to focus on the pieces that I wanted to be known for. I had to think about what I needed them to know.

When leaders are considering talent moves and promotions, they discuss the following key characteristics to evaluate a candidate's overall fit for a role:

- Results and Expertise
- Integrity and Values
- EQ: Interpersonal Understanding and Influence
- Organizational and Cultural Acumen

Results and Expertise

Your name has made it into the conversation because it's expected you have met the threshold for the first two characteristics, your Results and Expertise—that is, your ability to do the job. However, these assumptions are validated through those who know your work, either during the discussion if someone in the group knows, or following it if further validation must be sought. Further validation depends on the reputation of those making statements about you and how confident or passionate they are about your contributions.

Integrity and Values

Leaders consider if you represent the company's values and if you can be trusted to do the right thing when decisions of integrity confront you. Perceptions and water-cooler conversations weigh heavily here. This addresses the decisions you make and what you do when you think nobody is watching.

What's the grapevine buzz about you. What juicy things do people talk about behind your back? Does what you do and say support the company's values? Do the decisions you make consistently support those values, too? Could you pass the organizational litmus test?

EQ: Interpersonal Understanding and Influence

Two characteristics—EQ: Interpersonal Understanding and Influence, and Organizational and Cultural Acumen—represent your style and how you get things done.

As you move into roles of greater responsibility, leading others is usually required. How you work with, engage, motivate, and influence subordinates, peers, and leaders indicates what your interaction and leadership style will be going forward. Knowing yourself as well as understanding and caring about how your approach affects others show your personal awareness and potential.

Leaders want to know: Do people in the company like and respect you? Or have you burned bridges along the way?

Can you effectively influence others and lead them to meet the organization's goals?

Organizational and Cultural Acumen

Organizational and Cultural Acumen refers to your awareness of the political environment around you and how you navigate within it.

This is an important indicator of how you will fit in, of how you will work within the organizational structure and norms at successively higher levels. Are you aware of business relationships, how the hierarchy influences and operates? Are you aware of the business protocol as you move up the ladder? Have you built mentor or sponsor relationships at higher levels of the organization, the beginning of a potential network to help you?

The higher the levels you're being considered for, the greater the focus will be on, and weight given to, the qualities of Interpersonal Understanding and Influence, as well as Organizational and Cultural Acumen.

A clear vision will help you make strategic career choices and assist you in aligning others' perceptions with the career path you've set out to pursue.

I remember when I was mid-career and knew it was time to move into a new role. I took a job I had not discussed with my mentor. When he found out, he was upset with me. Why? Because he knew information I didn't know, and this role did not align with where he saw my potential. That's how I realized I didn't have a clear vision of what I wanted to do or be known for. Though I learned from that role, it did not establish the image I needed among leaders that led to moving up in the organization.

To summarize, you have to be known for your "what" and "how" as you distinguish yourself from others. You want to influence the awareness of others about you and your water-cooler image—that is, what people say about you in casual conversations or when your name comes up in a meeting.

Always keep in mind that perceptions are reality.

Brand Management Plan: Two Parts

The second part of being well-known is having a plan. The well-known brands you thought of earlier have a brand management plan. They're not wishing and hoping you will notice them. They don't operate on wishing for good luck.

Your professional brand management plan is comprised of these two parts:

- Personal Brand Development Plan
- Personal Brand Marketing Plan

Part 1: Personal Brand Development Plan

Once you define your vision, you have to work at achieving it. That requires a plan to build your skills and experience to fulfill your vision of your brand—that is, your brand promise. In effect, you turn your career path into a plan to gain the skills and experiences you need to advance.

Review the following questions as your starting point for this portion of your plan:

- What experiences and skills might I need in preparation for the next two or three steps on my career path?

- Am I doing everything I can in my current role to begin to build the necessary skills to advance?
- How would I evaluate myself on these skills at this point?
- What can I do to develop these skills and gain additional experience?
- Are there projects or teams I can volunteer for, either within or outside of my day-to-day responsibilities?
- Am I doing everything I can to do my best in my current role?
- What are key actions, milestones, and timeframes to help me reach my goals?

As you build your personal development plan, the performance evaluation process is a helpful resource. Your performance review should identify areas of strength you can continue to build on, as well as skills targeted for further development. Ideally, it includes specific actions (agreed on with your manager) so you can work on your development areas. These are your first priority, as your development in these areas will help improve your performance in your current role. From there, you will have the foundation and potential to move ahead. Be sure to embellish this list of actions with additional actions to broaden these skills.

When you have a strong foundation and track record of execution, you have actual deliverables that can demonstrate your capabilities. What matters are the contributions you make toward meeting the goals of your team, department, company, and customers. That means constantly developing your technical, interpersonal, and leadership skills. Accept that there's always something new to learn.

Part 2: Personal Brand Marketing Plan

Now that you've established your career goals and skill development priorities, it's time to work on the second part of your brand management plan: your brand marketing plan.

Your personal brand marketing plan has three primary objectives:

- Position Your Brand to Support Your Vision
- Create a Buzz
- Promote What You Want to be Known For

Personal Brand Marketing Plan, Objective 1:
Position Your Brand to Support Your Vision

"Walk the talk." Consistency is key here. The things you say and do need to support the potential you want others to see in you. This begins with demonstrating you possess the skills to deliver results in your current position. Just like dressing for the job you want, you also want to demonstrate you can be accountable and take on greater responsibility.

Your brand positioning also speaks through your emotional intelligence and your ability to build effective and respected interpersonal working relationships. Actions speak louder than words; they also speak more often than words. What you do to represent your brand will support or detract from your vision. When you have the opportunity to state your career goals and skills, be sure to share your strengths and experiences that relate to the future roles you'd like to grow into.

Consider This:

Do your actions and words support what you want your brand positioning to represent?

What do you want others to think about you?

Think of situations when your actions and words have *best* represented your brand and *least* represented it.

Personal Brand Marketing Plan, Objective 2:
Create a Buzz

Include opportunities for exposure in your personal brand marketing plan. Share your story to begin building a network of advocates who can speak highly of you. After all, people's experiences with you will largely dictate what they say about you. If you don't treat people well, the buzz about you will be negative. Again, actions speak louder than words.

Yes, you can be proactive about creating buzz. How? By sharing information about the projects you're working on, your role, your minor accomplishments, and your major achievements. Share notes of appreciation from peers, stakeholders, or leaders. Set up a regular status meeting with your boss so that sharing can become routine.

Also, set up sharing opportunities with mentors, internal clients, and stakeholders. Make sure the information you share demonstrates your influence on the business. Give them something worth telling others about. Remember, consideration for promotion focuses on "what" you get done, then "how" you get it done.

You're probably concerned about how you do this without coming off as over-confident or only talking about yourself all the time. Promoting yourself doesn't mean you have to talk about "me." Recognizing your team and your effort as part of that team can also be meaningful. It demonstrates your mindset as a team player. However, the team doesn't get promoted into a single position. Individuals get promoted. So take time to demonstrate the contributions and skills you *personally* bring to the team's success.

Melanie Shook offered examples of her strategies to create buzz:

> You have to be comfortable talking about yourself and promoting yourself. I know it was uncomfortable for me as I started doing that. I had to learn to be comfortable promoting myself.
>
> It's a delicate balance. I had to do it in a way that made me feel that I wasn't compromising my integrity or going into a space where I felt it was overbearing. I had to do it continually, and I had to do it often. There's no shame in participating, as long as, in my mind, I have something worthy of participating in. I wouldn't promote just anything. But, I felt like if I put my sweat equity into something that was worthy of promoting, then there's nothing wrong with sharing it.
>
> I would first start with my boss and make sure he or she had a clear understanding of my contributions. Because I work remotely from the corporate office, I had to work hard to make sure I was understood.
>
> I think it starts with direct managers and making sure they clearly understand everything you're doing.

I took for granted that they knew what I was doing, and I found out they had no idea. You have to open that level of communication with your immediate supervisor. Make sure there's a clear understanding of what you do so that person can represent you at the table. It's hard to promote something you don't know about. So a lot of it was starting a dialogue with my immediate manager, making sure there was a clear understanding of my contributions. I accomplished that through our one-on-one meetings we had every other week.

I made sure I was always bringing to the conversation ways to increase his awareness of activities I was working on. I definitely leveraged the formalized end-of-year processes we have and then the informal opportunities, too.

I've found that I'm very independent and just do things. And I expect that no news is good news, which isn't necessarily true. Sometimes I have to invite other people to not just *hear* the news but also *experience* it. I invite them to participate in activities, so they can see for themselves what's happening.

For example, I was on a call, and one of my colleagues said how much of a transformation she's seen in my group in the past couple of years. She'd been working closely with my team and could see the evidence herself. That spoke more loudly than anything I could say to her myself.

So, take a varied approach. But in the end, it helps to get other people to promote your platform, share what you are striving to work on.

You can assume people see what you're doing and automatically know about your contributions. But, as we learned from Melanie, that's not true. You have to speak up and tell your own story.

Personal Brand Marketing Plan, Objective 3: Promote What You Want to be Known For

Let me reiterate: Actions speak louder than words. Therefore, make sure your actions are consistent with what you want to be known for.

On an ongoing basis, consistently reevaluate the most important two or three messages you want to get across. These messages will relate to your results, your efforts in going above and beyond expectations, your unique ideas and solutions, potential opportunities, or new approaches to doing things. These messages are your brand promise.

Do you recall the brands that came to mind when discussing brand promise earlier in this chapter? The brand promises claimed by those companies must be delivered when you receive the product or service. Brand promises are not hollow. Similarly, your brand promise has to consistently demonstrate real substance to support your claims. Shallow or false promises are short-lived and can derail your career.

Your personal brand marketing plan involves doing the following to stand out from the crowd: earning a strong track record of "what" (your ability to execute) and "how" (your emotional intelligence); portraying an executive presence that shows professionalism and self-respect; sharing your contributions and accomplishments with others.

Do such a good job in your work that you have others singing your praise. That's the ultimate marketing *and* the most credible. Ralph de Chabert, the chief diversity officer for Brown-Forman Corporation, said:

> If you don't tell your own story by managing it, somebody is going to create a story for you. I don't really know your story until you tell it to me. Telling your story is terribly important, because someone else may write a different story for you.

Brand Trait #3: Perceived Runway

The third trait of a powerful brand is solid Perceived Runway. For professionals, Runway means that others see accelerating career potential in you. They can envision you in the future with greater responsibility and, potentially, in higher levels in the company. They'll test you to see if their theory holds true, but at least they begin to believe you have a promising future.

Remember, your ability to execute is foundational. Runway means you're expected to continue delivering value-added business impact with integrity in a way that has a positive influence within the organization. Nancy Torra has seen it in her own experience:

> I feel like companies are not only trying to see whether you can do the job. They're trying to see what else you bring to the table. Why are you so valuable? A lot of things can be learned, but it's about what else you have the potential to bring.

When leaders evaluate your Runway, they're assessing your future career growth potential in these areas:

- Ability to Deliver Results
- Integrity and Values
- Coachability
- Developing Skills and Competencies
- EQ: Emotional Intelligence
- Representing the Desired Company Image

Did you notice the word "coachability" appears on this list? Even as you move up in your career, you always have to be open to learn and grow. No one knows everything. Even senior leaders have mentors and peer groups they learn from. The most successful leaders seek feedback and have a mindset of continuous improvement. Because the world is in a constant state of change, organizations are forced to change, too. People are different, situations are different, and nothing remains as it was yesterday. This presents ongoing opportunities for awareness and learning.

Leaders assess your perceived ability to be a professional who can represent the company well. If you were with a client or in public, would the company be proud for you to represent what it wants to be known for?

As leaders discuss future leaders, they evaluate Runway from their knowledge and perceptions of you. If you haven't been developing and marketing yourself, you may be perceived as limited. It's not a static designation about you at a single point in time. Rather, it's continually evaluated against the ongoing needs of the business.

Kelly Schmidt offered this peek inside Johnson & Johnson's talent discussions on Runway:

> One thing I have heard repeatedly in our development conversations is, "Are they just that good because

that's their sweet spot and they've been doing it for so long? Or are they just that good in general?" That's one of the things we try to figure out, so we can identify where people are going to grow. Are they going to grow in a singular fashion? Or are they going to develop more broadly? It's really general management and general technology aptitude.

For example, if someone has been working in a particular space for a number of years, sometimes a watershed moment occurs. That's when you're given an activity that stretches you beyond your current capabilities. Let's say you've been working in a particular technology for a consumer. To have that one extra example that you're ready for a promotion, we'll try to find something in a different sector, yet in that same technology, so you still have something you're comfortable with. We want to see if you can apply what you know a bit more broadly.

Some of our succession plan "prep" conversations include talking about someone's career runway and what they can do. We talk about how many levels in the organization they could move in a year to five years. We also address the development activities that may line up against that to ensure getting to that level or a target job.

Perceptions of your Runway are formed by what people know or don't know about you. So consistently demonstrate your capabilities at every opportunity and share with others the work you're doing to help the business succeed.

Manage Your Reputation. It Matters.

You have more control over your reputation than you can probably imagine. It's important to remember you have to build a foundation for your reputation by delivering consistent over-the-top execution and by managing your brand. Managing each of the three traits of a powerful brand (Stand Out from the Crowd, Well-known, and Perceived Runway) will help you establish the type of Reputation you need to begin to FuelForward in your career. Otherwise, others will establish your reputation for you, like it or not.

This is the first level of your Career FuelForward Accelerators. Your moves from here will be less effective if you don't do the work to make other's perceptions become the reality you want to create. Strategies covered in the following chapter will help you reach your audience with your brand message.

●   ●   ●

REMEMBER:

⇒ Your reputation is vital to your ability to FuelForward your career. The information others have about you is the basis for their perceptions. Proactively building your personal brand in a way that will positively affect your career growth is not optional.

⇒ Your personal brand is your reputation. Your brand represents what people think about you. People take action and make decisions around what they believe to be true.

⇒ Your water-cooler image is the informal conversations people have about you that can influence your career without you even knowing it.

⇒ A powerful brand has three traits:
    1. Stand Out from the Crowd
    2. Well-known
    3. Perceived Runway

To Stand Out from the Crowd, you must:

⇒ Have a strong track record of "what" (your Results and Expertise) and "how" (your Emotional Intelligence and Leadership), and

⇒ Become recognized for your Professionalism and Executive Presence.

To be Well-known, you must have:

⇒ A Clear Vision of what you want to do, and what you want to be known for, and

⇒ A Brand Management Plan to manage your personal development and personal brand promotion.

To have Perceived Runway:

⇒ Others can envision you in the future with greater responsibility and, potentially, in higher levels in the company. To get their attention, be sure to walk the talk and tell your story.

Managing each of these three traits will establish the type of Reputation you need to FuelForward.

Resource:

What do you want to be known for?

Visit www.*FuelForwardBook.com/resources* to download a Reputation Strategy Planning worksheet.

Chapter Seven

FuelForward Accelerator: Reach

Reach has become more important, because there is not as clear a sense of where things are getting done as there once was. And people have so many things they focus on during each day, you won't be front of mind when an opportunity comes up, unless you have a good reputation and have fairly good visibility a level or two up from your own role.

–Katie Gaughan, President and Founder
  Point C Consultancy

Broadening Connections through Reach

Just a few years ago, political campaigns were primarily fought on national and local network television stations. Political parties and candidates would buy advertising space so their commercials could reach voters with their campaign messages. Candidates with the biggest advertising budgets could buy more advertising spots on more stations, thereby reaching more people.

Why has the battle of the airwaves been so important? Greater advertising reach means greater numbers of people are aware of those candidates and their positions on issues. This has brought people to the polls to vote for them on Election Day.

Today, national and local television ads are still important, with funds still being spent to reach voters. But not as many people watch television as they used to. Therefore, voters must be reached in a variety of ways through electronic and social media and by word of mouth. Regardless of the medium, making connections with voters and selling their messages is still the name of the game for politicians.

The term "Reach" refers to the total number of people or households exposed, at least once, to an advertising message during a given period. Politicians and advertisers are strategic about the types and numbers of voting constituents they reach through an optimal combination of online and offline media.

Careers are a lot like political campaigns. You have to reach a target audience of leaders and other professionals to make them aware of who you are and the brand you represent. Remember, your brand is represented by the track record of your execution and your character, and the impression you make as people observe and interact with you. Leaders make most hiring and promotion decisions based on whom they know, what they know about them, and what they believe to be their potential.

Similar to politicians, you have to take advantage of opportunities to build connections, to expand your Reach so you're on their minds when career-related decisions are made. Reach opens the door for greater awareness of your capabilities and skills in adding business value.

Reach, together with the Relationships that develop as a result, has the greatest effect on actual career advancement of any of the elements discussed in this book.

In my interviews, Ralph de Chabert said, "If you ask the question 'What does it take to grow in an organization?' it's this: You have to be known." Kelly Schmidt agreed. She said, "The exposure is not the first thing our organization thinks of. But the thing is, if you don't have that exposure, your reputation isn't cultivated. It doesn't matter what kind of results you've had if nobody else knows about it."

In this chapter, you'll learn to identify Reach opportunities you may not even recognize, whether you work in an office environment or remotely. You'll learn how to maximize Reach for career growth. You'll also find that Reach is transferrable outside of the workplace and can be extended to various playing fields.

Reach: Going Beyond Your Immediate Circle

Reach is the politicians' opportunity to increase their awareness among their constituencies. And Reach is the same for you and your career. Reach creates an extension of connections beyond the people who interact most closely with you on a day-to-day basis, both at work and outside of work. In fact, in today's environment, you'll find your Reach into the community, both physically and virtually, will be just as important in expanding your career options.

Reach provides a chance to broaden others' awareness of your capabilities and skills in adding value to the business. By intentionally broadening your Reach, you'll be exposed to people you may not otherwise come in contact with.

To move ahead, you want people to be exposed to the work you do and the value you contribute. You have opportunities at your fingertips that you may not be even aware of. It's through these opportunities of broadened Reach that you build your personal brand image.

Remember, no matter what element of career management you're working on, building your core to achieve a track record of solid performance execution is still the most important first step to advance your career. Strong performance won't necessarily get you promoted. However, you can't get promoted without it.

Leaders constantly assess who goes above and beyond. That naturally influences decisions about added responsibility, who is appointed to special project teams, or who is pinpointed for other opportunities. For you to be considered, leaders have to be aware of you and the value you add to the organization.

Ralph de Chabert shared how Reach influences closed-door discussions:

> Two conversations go on in those meetings. There is one conversation about people's performance, that they did X, Y and Z, and are courageous, collaborative and more. Another conversation relates to the relationships I have with each of those people.

Reach can have positive or negative consequences. Decisions you make about your visibility to and interactions with others will heavily influence the outcomes in your career. What people say about you during those closed-door discussions is due in large part to how you manage Reach.

Benefits of Reach

Reach offers three important benefits. First, it's an objective way to make connections, so that others become aware of your potential and recognize your business value. Still, you need multiple opportunities and venues to demonstrate your skill set.

Dr. Clayton Christensen, a Harvard Business School professor, used an example that captures this concept perfectly. He explained that various events and interactions in life are like movie clips—that is, you want people to be exposed to more than a random sampling of these clips. Therefore, you have to be intentional about making more of your movie clips visible, ensuring they fit together. Then they will give more visibility to who you are, what you can do and have done, and what you represent. Others need to be able to put those clips together and know your story.

Ralph de Chabert has seen this play out in the companies where he's worked. He said:

> How I interpret a person's performance is often very subjective. And the subjectivity is colored by my experiences. Therefore, you want to give people a different set of experiences with you. In doing so, they get comfortable and can advocate on your behalf.

Secondly, you can use Reach as a tool for implementing your personal brand marketing plan by demonstrating what you want to be known for. People already have an impression of you. Reach is one of the few ways to prove or disprove their assumptions.

Reach heightens awareness about you. It gives you the opportunity to control the message and reinforce your brand promise.

Finally, it may lead to the kind of connections that could earn leader sponsorship, which can be a critical advantage. As noted with Reputation, if people don't know you, they can't recommend you. Having someone advocate for you is a powerful builder of credibility.

Consider This:

How can these benefits of Reach help you?
- Reach broadens visibility about your potential and business value.
- Reach provides a strategic approach for executing your personal brand-marketing plan.
- Reach increases potential for sponsorship because more people know about you.

Types of Reach

Are you asking, "What can I do to broaden my reach?"

In a professional environment, you don't buy advertising to promote your brand's value. Instead, you can include three types of Reach in your career management toolkit. Remember, Reach includes the brand message you are sending or portraying as well as the number and type of people exposed to your brand. To develop an effective Reach, work on each of the three I's of Reach:

- Involuntary
- Intentional
- Invited

Involuntary Reach

Opportunities to extend your Reach abound in everyday situations. First, you are always being watched, so you never know when someone is observing your behavior or professionalism. Involuntary Reach occurs when people are exposed to you, but you are not thoughtful or aware of the impression you're making. They form perceptions as a result.

When I was little, sometimes I'd misbehave in the store if I couldn't get what I wanted. My mom would say, "Other people are watching you." I, in my own little world, didn't realize it, nor did I care at that age. She, of course, was embarrassed. I didn't realize how true that statement was until I had to use it with my own children. (It didn't necessarily work on them, either.)

Don't ever forget that you are always "on," whether in a casual or business environment, informal or formal. You're "on" when you're talking on the phone, chatting at the coffee pot, using the wrong tone in email, or drinking too much at a business or social function. Somebody may be watching or listening to you, and you don't even know it. The deepest opinions are formed when people see the real you, especially when they know you don't know they're watching you.

A friend recently told me an incident of Involuntary Reach becoming a negative brand impression. He was attending an important business meeting and happened to be in the restroom at the same time as a senior executive. He introduced himself as they were washing their hands. Just then, another man finished his business and exited the restroom without washing his hands. The senior executive commented how that person must lack self-respect and fail to pay attention to details. He actually commented that he wouldn't trust that person—*based on not washing his hands!* Yes, people notice you when you're the most unaware.

Involuntary Reach can occur in meetings as others make judgments about your involvement or lack thereof. Do you engage by providing input to the discussion or by asking questions? Do you welcome and respect the input and questions of others? Even if you don't say anything, you're making an impression.

Little things matter. You never realize who's watching you or the impression you're leaving, and you may never be aware of the consequence of that impression. Kimberly Black-Maffet, Associate Athletic Director for the University of Louisville, explained the result this way:

> Performance is absolutely critical. It has to be running on six cylinders all the time. You're being judged when you don't even know you're being judged. And unless you have a pretty good reason, if everything is expected to be 110 percent, then you've got to run at 110 percent.

Consider This:

What Involuntary Reach situations do you need to be made aware of? List two or three situations in which you could improve your involuntary outcomes.

Intentional Reach

Did you know you could create opportunities for Reach?

Like Involuntary Reach, you have a choice in the way you engage in everyday interactions with others. You create an impression from these interactions, which also affects your personal brand. Intentional Reach occurs by strategically increasing your involvement and aligning your actions with the outcomes you wish to achieve. It serves to broaden your connections and visibility.

Most professionals interact with so many people on an everyday basis that they give those interactions little thought. Don't be neglectful! Take care in how you work with people and support your project teams. Be intentional about aligning your actions with the values and integrity that will garner respect.

You can also create Intentional Reach by volunteering for activities outside of your job responsibilities. Seek special projects of importance to the business. Take advantage of volunteer opportunities. These projects can be inside or outside of your function or business unit. They could be broad business initiatives or community service projects. For example, volunteering for local non-profit organizations broadens your Reach in the community in a positive way. If you look, you'll find a wide variety of ways to get involved that suit your interests.

GE has an organization called GE Volunteers, which engages employees and retirees in serving their communities. Each GE business has a GE Volunteers chapter that organizes volunteer opportunities for its business unit and operating locations. A GE Volunteers chapter sponsors one or two large projects each year in which nearly all the employees participate. For example, they might complete a major renovation for a charitable organization in one day.

In addition, the GE Volunteers chapter encourages the business unit's departments and employee affinity groups to sponsor service projects within their groups throughout the year. They also provide opportunities to participate in activities such as mentoring programs and science fairs with local schools.

You can volunteer to be a participant, be on a planning team, or even serve as a project leader. Because these are important initiatives for the company, employees are usually encouraged to get engaged. Senior leaders are closely involved as executive staff sponsors of the company's volunteer organization and special projects.

Any of these opportunities connect you to other professionals and leaders from across the business community—people you might not get to work with otherwise. The events become venues to showcase your skills, including project management, leadership, and influencing. You also get a chance to develop additional skills and competencies, often in a low-risk environment.

One of the leaders I interviewed is a manager in a medical products company. She spoke about the importance of participating in events this way:

> These volunteer project committees are usually appointed by the CEO or a VP. It's constantly communicated on the intranet that this process is going on and what group of people is doing them. If they come to you and ask for help or advice or they request your time, please be willing to give it. The

work isn't that challenging. And it's all about working on a team and gaining visibility from doing that.

You could also create Intentional Reach by being intentional about making connections. For example, I'm an adjunct professor at the University of Louisville College of Business. Sometimes the College of Business has programs sponsored by a local company in which executives such as company CEOs give presentations and updates on their business, the economy, and different initiatives going on. These are optional events, but I always try to attend and support them to keep up with the topics. I also encourage my students to attend.

As I walked into one of these events, I saw my department chair. Then, I noticed some of my students in the room. So I put my folder down and walked over to the department chair to say hello. I made sure he knew I was there. I also mentioned some of my students were attending, even though I hadn't given extra credit for doing so. Some of them were simply interested enough to show up. That demonstrated to him what I wanted to reinforce in my personal brand: I'm present, I'm interested, I want to continue to learn and grow. And I'm supporting the department's initiatives.

The speaker at this particular event was the CEO of Humana Inc., a Fortune 100 healthcare company. His presentation generated a few questions in my mind, so I took the opportunity to ask them during the Q&A portion of the session. I was the first person to ask a question and the only one to stand up and introduce myself. After I gave my name, I mentioned I was a former Humana employee, having started my career there. I did this to make personal connections.

Getting out of my comfort zone and speaking up with a genuine inquiry helped me build a little more credibility. As a result, several people came up to speak with me after the program. But I didn't take either of these steps just for the sake of being seen. I sincerely wanted to speak to my department chair because I like and respect him, and I genuinely had questions for the speaker that I was curious about. I could have talked to my department chair later and mentioned my attendance. But taking advantage of an opportunity *at that moment in time* is what makes Reach more effective.

You often hear about having your elevator speech ready when you run into executives. One leader in the healthcare industry shares how she takes advantage of unique opportunities to extend her Reach:

> Professionals are encouraged to stop by the office of other directors who have products similar to yours and say, "We just finished this study about X. I don't know if you guys are interested, but I would be happy to come to your staff meeting to present. Or, I'd be happy to shoot you an email with the report." That way, they know what you've been working on, and you can be top of mind when they are recruiting for committees or other initiatives.

You'll be surprised how many Intentional Reach opportunities are available in your daily interactions. Look for them!

Professionals often say they don't have time to take on the types of volunteer roles or the extra initiative discussed in this section. If you want to move forward in your career, my question is this: "Can you afford not to?"

Consider This:

What Intentional Reach opportunities can you take advantage of? List one or two you have available to volunteer in and get involved. They can be either at work or outside of work.

Invited Reach

Invited Reach results from opportunities others make available to you. They broaden your visibility.

Primarily, Invited Reach opportunities are earned through the first two foundational elements of career advancement, your Execution and Reputation. If you make it to this stage in the game, leaders have some knowledge of your Execution (what) and your EQ or emotional intelligence (how). They believe you have a positive Runway, that you're ready to be tested among higher-level audiences and more business-critical situations. They're willing to give you a chance to demonstrate your talent and skills.

This often plays out as exposure opportunities in presentations, or in visible project leadership or functional leadership roles. Invited Reach also extends itself into the community. Look around at all of the community initiatives going on in your own backyard. People pull in those they know or have been recommended to get the job done.

The linkages between elements that open these opportunities were described well by Ralph de Chabert in this observation:

> My experience says if you perform, then you have greater degrees of freedom to get additional forms of exposure. So it's very much tied to performance. That much is real. It gives you the opportunity to participate on this task force, to engage in this employee resource group or other activities. Then people get to see you in different lights. You can look for those opportunities in the organization. One place where there is always more exposure and related opportunity is taking on those jobs and assignments others don't want to do, and then doing them well.

These Invited Reach opportunities are not to be taken lightly. Even though they are considered earned, they are a privilege—not a right. The leaders who invite you to these exposure opportunities are sticking their necks out. Sure, they have some level of confidence that you'll do a good job. But they're being judged on their ability to identify potential talent. How you do in these situations reflects positively or negatively on the leader who invited you to the dance.

Do you remember your senior prom in high school? Who invited you or whom you invited to the dance was just as important as what you wore. You were judged on the reputation and popularity of your date. Professional situations are similar. What's the track record and reputation of the person being invited to the exposure opportunity? Naturally, leaders select professionals who reflect positively on their image. You only get a chance to be invited if your image portrays a high-performing, high-potential professional.

Recognizing Invited Reach Opportunities

How do you recognize Invited Reach opportunities? Your boss may give you a chance to present at a meeting, or your project client or sponsor may provide an opportunity to give a project update in an all-employee call. You may be asked to lead a special project team or community service event or serve on a non-profit board. You may even be asked to provide a report that will be shared with other functions or leaders. You could be given additional responsibility in your current job or asked to take a visible functional leadership position.

Whether in person or virtual, all invitations are equally important. Some of these opportunities may seem small. You may not recognize them as an opportunity to broaden your Reach at all. These can turn into Involuntary Reach opportunities in which you're being observed and evaluated even when you're not aware of it. That's why it's important to always conduct yourself with the utmost professionalism. Be prepared to do your best for each and every interaction.

I remember when I worked for GE and was being looked at as a high-potential candidate for the next leadership level. We were attending one of the affinity group conferences our business unit CEO, human resource leaders, and other functional leaders would attend for a portion of the event each year. Human resources would host a special invitation breakfast or luncheon for high-potential candidates for the first-level ranks of executive leadership.

Each of us was being watched and evaluated in these ways:

- Were you punctual?
- Were you dressed professionally?
- Could you make small talk?
- Did you use proper etiquette at the table?
- Were you conversant on current business topics?
- Could you speak about your contributions to the business and future career aspirations?
- Would you be able to represent the brand image and values expected of its business leaders?

Their assessment of us during one of these events opened or narrowed future Reach opportunities.

During a project for one of my clients, I interviewed the office manager of a physician practice who was highly respected for her work. She shared that she'd been asked to go to each of the last three physician offices she's managed. They were all challenging situations, but ones that she turned around.

She told me about a lingering office issue that had never been resolved. "It's just the way it is," she'd been told. So she came in and got the team focused on the problem, resolving that issue in just a few weeks. She brought with her a strong foundation of adding value to the business. That generated visibility and influenced others' perceptions about her capabilities to solve seemingly unsolvable challenges.

This office manager built her reputation for strong "what" and "how" performance, for getting the job done while affecting the environment around her in a positive way. Her high level of consistent execution, the Reputation she developed as a result, and the attention she generated from Involuntary, Intentional, and Invited Reach created a buzz about her. That buzz led to a demand for her talent and opened opportunities for her. When I interviewed one of the physicians in her office, he raved about "how" she could lead, providing specific examples.

Consider This:
What Invited Reach opportunities have been made available to you? Did you recognize them as Invited Reach opportunities? What were the outcomes?

The experience of the office manager of a physician practice gives a perfect example of how this career management concept all comes together. No matter what your goals are—taking more responsibility in your job, moving into higher level roles, taking a lateral move to another business unit, or landing a role at another company—take advantage of all three I's of Reach: Involuntary, Intentional, and Invited.

Earning Invited Reach

Invited Reach is the type of Reach most out of your control, and it is earned. What can you do to increase your opportunities for Invited Reach?

First, work your brand management plan, both the development and marketing aspects. Leaders have to know you and believe you have the potential to do a good job with the opportunity they afford you. Make sure your execution is strong. Have a plan to work on your development areas, to assist you both in your current role and in subsequent roles on your career path.

Imagine that one of your goals is to run a marathon. You're going to have a training plan. You're going to consistently work through that plan to improve your performance, endurance, and speed. Your plan may include running shorter races to give you experience and prepare you for the big day. You wouldn't run a marathon without this type of preparation. Treat your professional skill development the same way, so you can optimize your execution and prepare a solid foundation of skills for future roles.

Then, work your personal brand marketing plan. If leaders don't know of your contributions and abilities, they can't advocate for you. Your brand promise must be solid. Leaders will eventually catch on to a shallow brand promise, which will potentially derail your career. It won't take long for them to figure out the chocolate bunny is really hollow. You don't necessarily get three strikes before you're out, professionally. Be proactive in sharing your contributions and accomplishments. Be sensitive to your approach. Don't come across as arrogant, and remember to recognize other teammates who may have contributed to the success.

Just as consumers have to build trust in the brands they purchase, leaders have to get to know you. They have to believe you have the potential to do a good job with any opportunity put in front of you, no matter how small or insignificant it may seem.

The third way to earn Invited Reach is to take advantage of the different types of Reach: the Involuntary, by making your character represent you well in all situations; and the Intentional, by adding value and volunteering for projects outside your day-to-day responsibilities, so others can become familiar with you.

Optimizing Reach Opportunities

Optimize Reach opportunities when you have them. Many of your Reach opportunities will come from demonstrating your skills or business acumen in a variety of situations or interacting with others across the organization. You want to use these opportunities to build your personal brand with positive impressions.

How do you do that? You can do two easy things: prepare, and get feedback.

Preparing for Reach Opportunities

Don't fall into the trap of thinking, "I've got this." Don't decide that a particular meeting or presentation is small-time and you don't need to worry much about it. If you try to wing it, or not prepare, the impression you make is not likely to come out well. Large or small, take the time to prepare.

To prepare, make sure you understand the expectations for the meeting, presentation, or report—whatever the format of your exposure. Be clear on the timeframe, location, dress code, format, length, audience, key messages, desired outcomes, and agenda. Ask questions to make sure you clearly understand. Don't assume you know.

Then, make sure you practice. During one of his presentations, motivational speaker Les Brown shares the importance of practice. He says that we're used to hearing, "Practice makes perfect. You don't have to be perfect. Practice makes you better." You have to practice to get better, be well prepared, and know your information. And, you can bet that practice will help you feel more confident and relaxed, which will help improve your execution and reputation.

Getting Feedback on Reach Opportunities

As you prepare, and after any of your exposure events, make sure you ask for feedback. Who would you get feedback from? Just like we talked about with your brand development plan, you can get feedback from your manager, mentor, trusted peers, or other leaders and associates you're working with.

What kind of feedback do you ask for? As you're preparing, ask for insight on the type of meeting: format, style, formality, tendency for questions. You also want insight on the audience, the format, and what has worked well or not so well. Be sure to gain information that will help you know what could happen when you walk in the room and how to add value to the business objectives.

Also, ask for feedback on your presentation or report content, format, delivery style, communication style, clarity of key messages, and demeanor. Ask what questions you should anticipate. Plan for questions. Write out your responses. Practice how you will respond so you won't come across as uninformed or defensive. Know the detailed information that supports your key points, so you can be prepared to answer questions and appear knowledgeable. When you don't know the answer to a question, you can say, "I don't know, but I will get that information for you," instead of providing an erroneous response. However, this response does not substitute for preparation.

Following your presentation, ask for feedback on your style, content, format, clarity of key messages, posture, demeanor, how you handled questions, and the overall impression of the audience. Use each experience as an opportunity to learn and grow. Be open-minded, so people will give you honest feedback. Reflect on the input you get and evaluate how you can improve. Know there's always room for improvement.

Rita Barksdale, a GE Healthcare executive, shared some advice from her experience:

> Be prepared. Do your due diligence before standing in the room. No matter how much work you put into it, a presentation can only be as great as it is to the person who receives it.
>
> Start by understanding your audience's purpose for the presentation. While you probably have clear objectives for it, various stakeholders in the audience may have additional needs you want to address. Understand the style of presentation that works best for them by speaking with your manager and peers as appropriate. Some may prefer presentations with 101 pictures on the page while others strictly text. Being aware of these variances will allow you to accommodate the different ways that people process data.
>
> Also, be sure to consider the whole audience. You want to build a presentation to the senior person but keep others engaged. Anticipate their questions. Brainstorm the types of queries you may receive from environmental health and safety, finance, human resources, etc., and be prepared. You could even run the presentation points by certain audience members in advance, if it's appropriate.

To reinforce why Reach matters, let me emphasize two important outcomes of Reach:

- Personal Brand Strength
- Sponsorship

Personal Brand Strength
What are the outcomes when Reach goes well?

You can have a significant effect on the traits of brand strength that we reviewed earlier: Standing Out from the Crowd, Well-known, and Perceived Runway. Leaders begin to increase their familiarity with you and confidence in you. You can grow into someone who's considered high-potential.

You'll continue to be observed for consistency in your "what" and "how," and for further validation of your reputation. As your familiarity and trust increase, leaders are more willing to be an advocate or sponsor for you, to speak about your track record and Runway when talent discussions arise.

What are the outcomes when Reach doesn't go well? Depending on the criticality and severity of the result, you risk decelerating or even derailing your career—especially if this happens more than once. Poor outcomes can establish a negative impression and possibly negative word of mouth. In the earlier stages of your career, you will likely get a few chances to make mistakes, learn, and grow. It's important to turn each mistake into a learning experience, as there's little tolerance for making the same mistake again and again.

The business can't afford the cost of repeated mistakes, and leaders will wonder if you lack the intelligence to learn or even care. Leaders aren't willing to risk their reputations as advocates for someone who repeatedly fails to do well.

Your performance reflects on them. Would the coach of a sports team continue with the same play and players if it failed to help the team win the game?

Entitlement doesn't win in sports or in business.

Sponsorship

What is a sponsor, and how does it differ from a mentor?

Sponsors, often called champions, are usually senior-level leaders who hold a level of influence in the organization. They become your promoters or ambassadors, speaking up about your track record and the capabilities they see in you.

Sponsors are earned. They have to get to know you and believe you have potential before they will become a sponsor. The degree of certainty and passion they have when they speak about you will heavily influence the perception of others.

You may have no sponsor or different sponsors along your career. Over time, players in the organization will change. Continue to work at generating Reach over the course of your career, so you can have the potential for sponsorship as the organization evolves.

In contrast, a mentor is someone who specifically helps you with your development areas. A mentor can be senior to you, a peer, or even a subordinate. Usually a specific learning or development objective is agreed upon.

A mentor may or may not become a sponsor. Just because a mentor has been working with you does not mean he or she will, or is even in a position, to advocate for you. (Learn more about mentoring relationships in my mini-book *Creating an Effective Mentoring Relationship*.)

Consider This:

Sponsors, or champions, are your promoters or ambassadors who will speak up about your track record and the capabilities they see in you.

Who has been a sponsor to you?

How have sponsors helped your career?

Why You Need a Sponsor and How to Get One

The office manager of a physician practice I interviewed is a good example of how sponsorship works beneficially. Once she proved herself by having a strong effect on the business, she began to get sponsored into other roles. People were asking her to take on other jobs. They knew they could depend on her to deliver. That's usually how that works—not 100 percent of the time, but most often.

As a leader considers talent, she thinks, "Who do I know who can come in and take care of this? I'm going to ask the people I know and trust to recommend someone." Your sponsors will be thinking of you at times like these. They will mention your name. Sometimes you won't even know about it!

How do you get a sponsor? Some leaders I interviewed strongly stated you *don't ask* someone to be a sponsor. Sponsors are earned. A sponsorship develops from interactions with you and consistent exposure to your movie clips that build trust in your ability and potential. Sponsorship grows from the human psychological response that builds as someone gets to know you, becoming comfortable and familiar with who you are and what you represent—your brand promise.

Other leaders believe you should advocate for yourself and *ask* a specific leader to be a sponsor. You don't just wait on the sideline to be put into the game. Let the coach know you're ready and that you want in. If you use this approach, articulate where you'd like to go in your career, the skills you hold and those you're building, and the track record of execution you bring to the table.

However, only ask a leader who is familiar and comfortable with you. You don't want to put others in an uncomfortable position when they have doubts or questions about you. This issue is extremely delicate, so proceed with caution. The more you gain exposure in your business by creating Reach opportunities and building credible relationships, the more people will know what you can do. Then more people will trust that you're someone who delivers.

Sometimes, you may not even realize you have a sponsor. A sponsor can be aware of you without having a direct connection with you personally. But, any awareness of your capabilities, style, and track record gives your potential sponsor reason to believe you have a solid Perceived Runway. If you have credible, trusted relationships, you increase your chances of having a sponsor like this.

Realize that the more people know about you, the more comfortable they will feel recommending you. When people recommend you, their necks are on the line. People who trust them trust their recommendations. You become a reflection on them. If you know people have recommended you for something, you owe it to them to do your very best.

Kimberly Black-Maffet shared her perspective on engaging a sponsor this way:

> You have to be discerning when you call upon people. At the inception of an opportunity, you want to have someone you'd like to carry your brand say, "Yes, I'm familiar with this brand. She's a wonderful person. This is her talent. I think this is what you'll get if you hire this person." But, also be wise and use that only when you must. Do not overuse it, because if you continually ask your sponsor to carry your message, at some point you lose your own credibility.
>
> And certainly, never ever have a sponsor be an excuse. I would never ask someone to speak on my behalf if I'd messed up something or disappointed someone or did not perform effectively. That can wreck your brand in one swoop.

Having a sponsor is a privilege. If you know someone has recommended you, always thank him or her graciously. Remember, nobody owes you anything.

Reach: A Tool, Not a Trump Card

Remember this point: Using Reach in an attempt to get exposure is not about trying to be an opportunist and meaninglessly getting in front of influential leaders. There's no substance in that. Rather, as said earlier, Reach is an earned privilege.

Your performance and worth, your worthiness, come first—without question. Reach can backfire on you if, because of lackluster performance, your foundation of

Execution and Reputation aren't in place. Reach is only relevant if you can live up to your brand promise. It helps you with broadened opportunities because of the innate nature of human beings. Simply stated, we're more comfortable with what we know, just like the respected brands you purchase every day.

You have control over your Involuntary and Intentional Reach opportunities and what you portray. They increase people's knowledge and trust of your potential, and possibly open up Invited Reach opportunities.

You can influence the outcomes of Invited Reach opportunities by doing everything you can to make sure they go well. Reach has a significant effect on advancing your career. Managed wisely, it can open doors to forming important strategic relationships. The next chapter focuses on these relationships.

●   ●   ●

REMEMBER:

⇒ Reach increases your potential to be top of mind when career-related decisions are being made.

⇒ Reach extends your connections beyond the people who interact most closely with you on a day-to-day basis.

⇒ Reach includes the brand message you are sending or portraying, and the number and type of people exposed to your brand.

⇒ Reach can have positive or negative consequences.

⇒ You need to build on each of the three I's of Reach in your career: Involuntary, Intentional, and Invited.

⇒ Involuntary Reach occurs when people observe you without your being aware of the impression you're making. People form perceptions as a result.

⇒ Intentional Reach occurs when you broaden your visibility by strategically increasing your involvement and aligning your actions with the desired outcomes.

⇒ Invited Reach occurs when others open doors to expanded opportunities.

⇒ Optimize these Reach opportunities to build your personal brand and make positive impressions.

⇒ Managed wisely, Reach can broaden your connections, setting the stage for forming important strategic relationships over time.

Resources:

How can you build on the three I's of Reach to extend your strategic connections? You're invited to visit www.FuelForwardBook.com/resources to download a Reach Strategy Planning worksheet.

Check out the mentoring guide *Getting the Most from Your Mentor*. Visit www.FuelForwardBook.com/resources to download.

Chapter Eight

FuelForward Accelerator: Relationships

Even though we have 40,000 employees nationwide, I feel like we have to maintain those good relationships. I always say don't burn any bridges.

I have seen that so much when I go from one department to the next, and I run into the same people. I'm like, "Oh my gosh, I'm glad I always had good relationships with these associates because otherwise, I would feel uncomfortable now."

You never know whom you're going to be working with. You never know who can recommend you. And when you interview, it might be somebody who knows somebody who knows you. And they may say, "Hey, I actually had a problem with that person a couple of years ago." People remember that.

I try not to take it personally when we have conflicts at work. They happen. It's natural. Handle them as best as you can and don't take it personally. It doesn't matter if you think, well, I'm not going to be at this company forever. You don't want to burn bridges. Instead, you want to maintain a good relationship because you don't know when you're going to need that person. I've been in a situation of needing something urgently. I've been able to pick up the phone and call someone, because I know that person will help me out.

Obviously, it's a two-way street, so develop that relationship in which you offer help and are always there when they need you. I know that if somebody called my previous business partners or co-workers, they wouldn't have complaints or anything negative to say about me—which is always good.

People talk before you get hired and before they give you a special project. They want to know they can trust you. When I move into a new role, I feel like people can trust me because they have seen my work ethic before, and I've been able to maintain those close relationships. That's very important.

–Nancy Torra, Project Manager

Building Credible Relationships

Have you ever heard the saying, "It's not what you know, but who you know?" Certainly, "what you know" is critical in your ability to get the job done. Your credibility begins with what you know and what you do with that knowledge. But what you know will only get you so far.

"Who you know" expresses the significance of people in the world around you. Imagine you plan to have a party. Your knowledge of party planning will help you plan a great event. But it's the *people* who make it an event. The more people you know, the more you can invite. Who attends your party has a lot to do with who knows you. If people don't know you well or at all, they're not likely to attend.

Yet, "who you know" implies a one-sided view of the relationship and overstates the level of significant influence you have on a relationship. Have you ever run into someone you met a few months before, walked up to say hello, and discovered they don't remember you? Until they know you, the real value of knowing them is limited. Once someone knows you, you can build on that mutual familiary and bring greater value into knowing each other. That common saying should be, "It's not who you know, but who knows you."

144

> ## Consider This:
>
> People often only think about building the volume of their network. A network can be a list of people you know. It's not *who you know* but *who knows you*, what they think about you, and the value that comes from knowing each other. That's why it's important to work on building your *relationships* and not simply a network.
>
> Have you focused on the numbers of people in your network or the value of the relationships?

The potential value of who knows you is influenced by what people know and think about you. People have various opportunities to interact with you. Their interactions with you are like short movie clips giving them a glimpse of who you are, what you are like, and what you do. Through these glimpses, people form an impression of you. They decide whether they like you or not, determining if you're someone they want to know better and have in their network.

Your opportunity to extend your connections with people begins at this early stage. Have you heard the saying, "First impressions are lasting?" The impressions set at this stage dictate the breadth, power, and potential of your network.

Relationships: Critical to FuelForward

Just like your personal life, your work life revolves around the people you interact with every day. They are your direct coworkers and team members, peers in other departments, internal client groups, business leaders, and customers. Each person in the organization has some level of influence on decisions, on other people, and directly or indirectly, on your career.

A person's influence on organizational decisions is typically based on the type of job she has or her level in the hierarchy. But, positional power is not required to influence other people's decisions, beliefs, and perceptions.

As leaders make staffing decisions, they want to feel confident they are making a solid choice. Their considerations will be based on either *who they know* or a recommendation from *someone they trust*. People influence each other based on relationships and a track record of honesty. Can I trust you and your judgment? Can I trust you because of the type of relationship we have?

The way the selection game works is a reflection of our natural tendencies as human beings. We rely on knowledge, and we need to feel comfortable when making critical decisions. Remember when you were a kid and picking the teammates for your kickball team? Who did you choose? Your buddies first, then the kids you knew were good at the game. Then, your buddies helped you choose from the kids who were still standing there waiting to be picked. It's no wonder we still use this same approach as adults.

The more you expand your network and build relationships inside and outside of your organization, the greater your opportunities for career growth.

There are generally four types of professional relationships:

- Acquaintances
- Allies

- Advocates
- Adversaries

Acquaintances

Acquaintances are people you've met; you know their names. They may be folks you've worked with on a project team or seen in your department from time to time. You haven't really worked closely together, so you don't know a lot about each other. You may cordially say hello when you see each other in the hallway.

Acquaintances are people you met at a networking event or when volunteering for a community organization. You generally glean a first impression of each other but not much more.

Allies

Allies are people you've had multiple opportunities to work or interact with. You've come to know each other and work well together. You know what to expect and have a respect for each other. You may sometimes connect socially, either at work or on a personal basis.

With your closest Allies, you tend to watch out for each other. You have each other's back. You often consider your closest Allies your friends, as well. Allies are helpful in getting your day-to-day work done. As reliable resources, they can provide a safe space for honest feedback, sharing ideas, and staying informed about organizational matters.

Advocates

Advocates are people who, though not necessarily Allies, know enough about you to have a high perception of you.

They've had opportunities to work with you or observe you, trusting that your track record is reliable.

Advocates believe you'll continue to add value in a constructive, meaningful way. They speak favorably about you and your work. They can become a sponsor, willingly mentioning your name and making favorable comments when they matter most. Often, you don't even know that someone is an Advocate.

Adversaries

Adversaries can have a significant influence on your career, so manage these relationships well. They are people who don't like you, don't get along with you, and usually don't want to work with you.

Adversaries may speak negatively about you to others, whether their statements are based on facts or not. They might create barriers to getting your work done, cause conflict, or be uncooperative when you need their assistance. Be aware of your Adversaries.

These relationship categories are not necessarily mutually exclusive. Overlap occurs. For example, Allies are sometimes Advocates, and Acquaintances can be Adversaries.

Remember, different types of relationships exist both at work and outside of work, and each one is extremely important to your career. Therefore, it's your responsibility to manage and develop them.

From Reach to Relationships

As you broaden your Reach, you're making others aware of who you are and your brand positioning. In the process, you're expanding your number of Acquaintances. That's a great starting point. You need to make sure that people are aware of you. But you have to work on turning some of those Acquaintances into Allies and Advocates.

Allies and Advocates are important to your ability to execute effectively and advance your career. Make sure your network inside and outside of your organization includes Acquaintances, Allies, and Advocates. It will also include some Adversaries, but you'll learn to manage the adversarial relationships just like you manage any other relationships. You will minimize the number of Adversaries as well as their influence on you professionally.

Consider This:

Make a list of important strategic connections you need to build.
- Who are the individuals?
- What are their roles?
- What types of relationships do you want to build or transform with them?
- What opportunities do you have to extend a helping hand to each person?

What are important relationships you need for effective execution and career advancement—key people to include in your Reach? Make a list of important strategic connections and jot down what type of relationship you need to build with each one.

Now, I don't pose this question for your selfish benefit. We don't "give" to "get." Relationships, even Acquaintances, should benefit both parties involved. You may even extend a helping hand to someone and never get anything directly in return. However, make sure your intentions in building relationships are genuine and let connecting with others for a purpose always drive your agenda.

Do you have people who call themselves friends, yet you only hear from them when they need something? How do you feel when people reach out to you like that? You feel less likely to help, or you feel like you're being used. So work on building your relationships *before* you need your network. When you connect with no hidden agenda, people are much more likely to help when the need arises.

Naturally, most relationships begin as Acquaintances. It's human nature to decide whether we like him or her—that's automatic. Of course, it will take time for you to get to know each other or work together. Similarly, it will take time and work to move those Acquaintances to Allies.

As relationships develop, there is a progression. Where the progress leads is based largely on your effort to reach out and show a genuine intent. The progression is not necessarily linear, however.

Although every relationship is two-way, it is 100 percent your responsibility to build the ones you want and make them work. For example, Ryan, a mid-level manager in a Fortune 1000 company, is intentional about creating Allies and Advocates. When he walks through the building on his way to a meeting, he makes it a point to say hello to people he knows. Sometimes, that leads to introductions to people he doesn't know. People tend to like Ryan, because he reaches out, shows a concern, and makes the conversation about the other person, asking how they're doing or what they're working on.

Many of your Acquaintances may remain Acquaintances for a long time. But the more you connect with them, the more you reach out to see what you can do for them, the more they know about you. The more they have opportunities to connect with you, the more opportunities they have to become a strategic partner in your network. This is how they become Allies and Advocates.

Nurturing relationships from Acquaintances to Allies or Advocates takes work. Remember, it's your responsibility, just like working on your career. Keep those connections going. People have to know what you're doing, what value you're adding, and who you are. Over time, they get exposed to your "movie clips." The more they see, the more they'll know about you. They become familiar with you and move through the relationship continuum.

Leveraging Reach to Build an Internal Relationship Network

There are natural opportunities to use Involuntary and Intentional Reach to broaden your visibility and build your network of relationships within the organization. Every day, you work in teams on projects with people in your department. Relationships with peers can go a long way to assist in your career. Reach out and introduce yourself to team members you don't work with closely. Let people know who you are. Say hello as you pass in the hallway. Treat people respectfully and take responsibility for what you're supposed to do.

Are there ways you can help other people? Without losing focus on your primary responsibilities, look for opportunities to extend a hand when others ask for assistance. After all, you may need their help some day. It goes both ways.

You could start conversations and make the subject about them, not you. For example, ask a coworker about his weekend. Find a common interest like sports, art, or community organizations that have common goals. Inquire about projects he's working on and show a genuine interest in how his meeting or presentation went.

Suzie knew that a couple of her teammates played on a softball team. She had played softball when she was in high school, so she'd often ask about their games or how the season was going. They would all have a good laugh reminiscing about the good old days and telling stories about their young athleticism. Suzie became a resource that her peers began to partner with more frequently on projects. These presented new opportunities that also extended her Reach to other professionals in the company.

Use Intentional Reach by taking advantage of opportunities to volunteer for special project teams outside of your department. Reach out to individuals and be proactive in making new Acquaintances. Find out a little bit about what people do, who they are, and their areas of expertise. When you need resources and expertise, you'll have more knowledge of who might help you. When you have a genuine interest in getting to know someone, you have the opportunity to share something about yourself, as well. More people know you and how you may be able to help.

Intentionally reach out and extend yourself by being part of special interest groups, employee affinity groups, or employee resource groups. By being part of those associations, you'll have opportunities to build relationships with people you would not otherwise.

You'll find that as you're meeting people, some won't share a lot of personal information or build personal relationships with people at work. That's okay, and it doesn't mean you can't be Allies with them. With those individuals, focus on building a deeper alliance in your work relationships and focus less on personal details.

Leveraging Reach to Build Relationships Outside of Work

Reach can help you build relationships outside of work in many ways. Look for organizations related to your field of expertise. Go to their meetings to meet other professionals in your field. Take advantage of their professional development programs. Attend their networking and social events, opportunities to get to know people in a more casual environment. Perhaps volunteer for them.

Also, locate non-profit organizations looking for volunteers to serve in the community. You may be invited to serve on a board or committee. Whatever you do, make sure you're genuinely reaching out to get to know people, not just ask what they can do for you. How can you help others?

Consider This:
List one or two Reach strategies that can help you expand your network of Acquaintances and build on other existing relationships within your network.

Managing Adversarial Relationships

It's important to know who your Adversaries are and understand why they are Adversaries. It's as important to manage adversarial relationships as it is to manage other kinds of relationships.

First, understand why the individual is an Adversary. You can give most people the benefit of the doubt. They probably have the best interests of the organization at heart, including yours.

However, sometimes Adversaries have hidden agendas that compete with yours from an organization or function standpoint or a personal, professional, or career standpoint. They may feel a bit of competition and believe there's only room for one person to excel or to move up.

As you look at your adversarial relationships, take time to make two decisions. One, is there anything I can do to turn this relationship around? Two, is it worth the effort to turn this relationship around?

As you consider the second question, make sure you're answering it not just for the "what can this person do for me" benefit but reciprocally. Is there something you can do for your Adversary? Also ask, "What difference does the working relationship between the two of you make to the organization?"

Consider This:

As you evaluate adversarial relationships, ask yourself:
- What can I do to turn this relationship around?
- Is it worth the effort to turn this relationship around?
- What difference does this working relationship between the two of us make to the organization?

Try to understand why adversarial relationships exist. Reflect on things that happened—conversations, times when you've worked together—to see if you have individually contributed to the conflict. If you can, take responsibility for your actions. Don't be the victim of the situation. Take the initiative. Determine what you can do to resolve the differences. Sometimes you have to swallow your pride and apologize for something you did.

Always be honorable in your relationships. Don't create adversarial tension with others. Are you as cooperative, attentive, or supportive as you could be? Are you working in a silo, or do you support teams cross-functionally to get work done? Are you in the game because you want what's best for the organization? Or are you taking advantage of situations to benefit only yourself?

Sometimes you see what you want to see in the mirror, not reality. Therefore, you may need to ask for honest feedback from someone you trust. If you are truthful with yourself and realize you're a part of the problem, then take steps to change the way you work. How can you be a help rather than a hindrance? Be part of the solution instead of the problem.

If you still find yourself on the unfortunate receiving end of the Adversary, consider these additional strategies:

- Over-prepare for interactions with the Adversary. Anticipate the person's potential objections in the meeting and prepare a response. Talk with trusted Allies before the meeting to discuss what objections may arise and why.
- Build consensus with others outside of meetings or before a major decision is finalized. Make sure you

have the opportunity for others to objectively hear the facts and your point of view.

- Talk to others after a meeting to get their perspectives on what influence the Adversary had on others in the meeting. Seek guidance on how to minimize that influence.
- Strategically minimize how often you interact or associate with the Adversary.
- Make sure other Acquaintances, Allies, and Advocates know you—your intentions, your contributions, your value, your competencies.
- Before you make people aware of the challenges between you and the Adversary, look in the mirror first. If you are simply fueling the fires of conflict, this decision will backfire on you.
- Engage a mentor who can help you navigate the politics of the organization, someone who can suggest strategies to minimize the negative consequences of the troubled relationship.

From Acquaintance to Ally to Advocate

Relationships progress through four stages over time and not always in a linear fashion. This progression establishes the foundation of credibility you need to achieve the levels of Allies and Advocates in relationships.

Think of the people in your inner circle. You know them well and enjoy spending time with them. You have mutual respect and trust. As you expand your Reach, getting to that point in your professional relationships requires progressing through these four stages:

1. Familiarity
2. Likability
3. Respect
4. Mutual Trust

Consider This:

On the road to credibility, relationships will evolve through the stages of Familiarity, Likability, Respect, and Mutual Trust. Reflect on how your relationships have moved through these stages.

Involuntary and Intentional Reach can help others become familiar with you. They will naturally decide if they like you. Being likable doesn't mean you're brown-nosing, being soft, or trying to please everyone. Sometimes you have to make tough decisions, but please be fair. People will trust and respect you for being tough and fair. Being likable means you find a common interest with someone. It means you treat others with respect and do your part to work well together on a team.

Repeated interactions and favorable, consistent outcomes help relationships evolve toward mutual respect and trust. People will evaluate their professional relationships with you based on questions like these:

"Do we share a common value system?"

"Are her behaviors and actions consistent, and as I expected?"

"Are the outcomes of our interactions as I expected?"

"Does he have the best intentions at heart?"

"Can I count on her to do a good job?"

"Can I expect him to represent me well if I give a recommendation?"

Leaders I interviewed emphasized that 99 percent of the time, as they select subordinates for promotions or special assignments, they don't intend to select only people from within their personal circle. But, it's human nature to feel more comfortable with people they know and respect. As a result, leaders are more likely to recommend someone they trust can live up to their claims. This protects their reputation.

The challenge for leaders, though, is building professional relationships with a diverse array of interests, talents, and cultures instead of simply selecting people who are most like them. Ralph de Chabert explained how this instinctive need to know someone plays out in a leader's decision-making process:

> People trust people they know. If I don't know you, yet you're expecting me to move you along pretty quickly, that's hard. When a manager has been able to take a risk with person A, it's because the manager has seen the person's work over time, or they've socialized together, or gone golfing together, or whatever. They believe they know the person. All of this gets complicated with the younger folks coming in. A leader may not know them, yet the leader is being asked to take risks, or these new hires may become impatient and leave. That can be a challenge for managers, especially when they have had little exposure to them or their working styles.

Relationships are two-way streets. People want to be around others who treat them with respect. Giving respect will get you respect in return. Yes, the Golden Rule really works: "Treat others as you would like to be treated." What value can you add by sharing information or making connections that help others grow and reach their goals? How can you be a resource to others?

Consider this question Darren Hardy poses in his book *The Compound Effect*: What percentage of shared responsibility do you have in making a relationship work? Complete responsibility. *Only when you are 100 percent responsible will a relationship work.*

Consider This:

Think about the professional relationships you have right now. Rate yourself on a scale of 1 to 5 on the following statements, with 1 for Disagree and 5 for Agree.
- I proactively reach up to build greater familiarity with those above me.
- I proactively reach broadly to engage a diverse array of individuals in my network.
- I proactively make contact, building connections and being a resource to others.
- I proactively take 100 percent responsibility for building trusted, credible relationships.

Relationships are critical to moving your career forward. It's incumbent on you to make the effort so the other person knows he or she is important. If you want others to recommend you, then you have to be 100 percent responsible for building trusted, credible relationships.

Think about the professional relationships you have right now. Do you proactively reach up to build greater familiarity with those on levels above you in your organization? Do you reach broadly to engage a diverse array of individuals in your network? Are you proactive in making contacts, building connections, and being a resource to others?

●   ●   ●

REMEMBER:

⇒ It's not only "what you know" or "who you know," but "who knows you."

⇒ There are generally four types of professional relationships: Acquaintances, Allies, Advocates, and Adversaries.

⇒ Reach will open the door to important professional relationships, both inside and outside of work.

⇒ You have to manage adversarial relationships, just as you have to manage all other types.

⇒ Strengthen your network by moving Acquaintances to Allies and Advocates.

⇒ To establish credibility, relationships must progress through the stages of Familiarity, Likability, Respect and Mutual Trust.

Resource:

What strategic relationships do you need to build into your professional network? Download your free Relationship Strategy worksheet by visiting *www.FuelForwardBook.com/resources.*

FuelForward

Chapter Nine

FuelForward

Your Insider's View

The race is on, and you're well on your way. You've got the insider's view of what it takes to FuelForward.

Now remember and apply these key principles:

Your career is not a sprint. Your career might span the better part of 30 years. What's the rush? To generate sustainable success, develop yourself, contribute, and prove yourself time and again. It just works that way. You gain credibility and new opportunities as you repeat the cycle.

You are the responsible party. *You* are the author and owner of your career. Nobody will be looking out for you all the time. Looking out for one career is enough!

The whole rather than the parts. The three E's (Expertise, Experiences, Execution) and three R's (Reputation, Reach, Relationships) work together as a system. Your success will stagnate if you try to use different components in isolation.

Bodybuilder approach. You can't succeed without a strong core or foundation. Make sure you consistently work on your Foundation (Expertise and Experience), so you can Execute at your best and live up to what you say you can do.

You'll be more effective as you launch the FuelForward Accelerators because you'll have a solid base to accelerate from.

What got you to this point in your career won't necessarily be enough to get you to the next level. Though the Foundation, Execution, is vitally important, Execution *alone* won't get you to the next level. To fuel your career forward, put into play and manage the FuelForward Accelerators (Reputation, Reach, and Relationships).

Reputation: Perception is reality. Does your brand represent you? If they don't know differently, people believe their perceptions about you are true. So tell your story. Reputation fuels the opportunities for Reach and Relationships.

Reach out and touch. Reach broadens the awareness and credibility of your brand, affording you the opportunity to FuelForward. Your career strategy will include the three I's of Reach: Involuntary, Intentional, and Invited. Manage all three.

Relationships: Who knows you? People can't advocate for people they don't know about. Of the four types of relationships (Acquaintances, Allies, Advocates, and Adversaries), focus on growing your network of Allies and Advocates. Relationships develop over time through four stages: familiarity, likability, mutual respect, and trust. Reach can lead to interactions that allow you to progress through these four stages. Only then can you earn the right to have Advocate relationships.

Don't regard these strategies as a one-shot deal. Rather, build a plan that's right for you and work on it every month, every week, and every day. Applying these practices doesn't require much extra time. Soon it will become second nature to you.

Don't get hung up on if what you're doing is exactly right, or if it's different from what someone else does. Your plan will be uniquely yours based on what's important to you. You'll learn and adjust along the way.

Find a buddy you can share this journey with—someone to be your cheerleader. Despite your efforts, you'll have frustrations and times when things don't go your way. You'll celebrate victories—both small ones and big ones. Having a buddy as a sounding board can help you stay on track.

If you'd like to go beyond this book and build a discipline around the model presented here, I can help. The keynotes, training workshops, coaching, and exercises I've created have helped countless professionals succeed.

I encourage you to maintain a steady pace and keep moving ahead. Others may fall out of the race, but not you. You're now able to FuelForward

About the Author

About the Author

Vivian Hairston Blade is a recognized author, experienced keynote speaker, corporate trainer, career coach, and executive coach on the principles of Leadership, Professional Development, and Talent Development. Her passion is building leaders and developing excellence in both organizations and individuals, enabling them to perform at their best.

Vivian has become a trusted advisor due to her foundation of deep, firsthand experience in the business world. She successfully climbed the corporate ladder, beginning her career as a management intern with Humana Inc., and reaching the executive level at General Electric.

Vivian currently works with some of the world's largest and most respected organizations—Proctor & Gamble, Brown-Forman, Johnson & Johnson, and others—to develop the talent they need to stay ahead in the marketplace. She also works with professionals on achieving their full potential and career goals. As adjunct professor at the University of Louisville's College of Business, she equips the next generation of professionals to start successful careers.

Vivian's professional certifications include GE Certified Lean Six Sigma Master Black Belt, Certified Project Management Professional, Certified Net Promoter Associate,

CRMI Certified Customer Experience Management Professional, ATD Training Certificate, and ATD Consulting Skills Certificate.

Vivian holds an MBA and a BS in Business Administration. Her professional memberships include National Speakers Association, Association for Talent Development, Customer Experience Professionals Association, Project Management Institute, and American Society for Quality.

Bibliography

Beeson, John. Getting that First Promotion. *Harvard Business Review*, March 18, 2013.

Brown, C.L. Victory over Rutgers shows Louisville football's Cards are a tough bunch of birds. *The Courier-Journal*, November 30, 2012.

Bureau of Labor Statistics, 2013 Earnings and Unemployment Rates by Educational Attainment, March 2014.

Bussey, John. "How Women Can Get Ahead: Advice from Female CEOs." *The Wall Street Journal*, May 18, 2012.

Bussey, John. "Women, Welch Clash at Forum." *The Wall Street Journal*, May 4, 2012.

Catalyst. Pyramid: Women in S&P 500 Companies. New York: Catalyst, January 13, 2015.

Chenault, Kenneth. 4 Tips for Career Advancement, Vault Blogs, January 25, 2011.

Chenault, Kenneth. American Express CEO Kenneth Chenault: Valuing EQ over IQ, Knowledge@Wharton, November 8, 2013.

Civilian labor force by sex, 1970 – 2012, Bureau of Labor Statistics, Current Population Survey / Graph by the Women's Bureau, U.S. Department of Labor.

Education and Synthetic Work-Life Earnings Estimates, American Community Survey Reports, U.S. Census Bureau, 2011.

Graduate-Degree Jobs With $100K Salaries, *US News & World Report*, March 11, 2011.

Groysberg, Boris, L. Kevin Kelly, and Bryan MacDonald. The New Path to the C-Suite. *Harvard Business Review*, March 2011.

Hardy, Darren. *The Compound Effect: Jumpstart Your Income, Your Life, Your Success.* Vanguard Press, 2011.

Karsan, Rudy. You Are The CEO Of Your Career. IBM Kenexa Smarter Workforce initiative blog post. 2014.

McGregor, Jena and Pam Tobey. Glass-ceiling update: A snapshot of women in leadership positions. *Washington Post*, Jan. 9, 2014.

Peters, Susan. How GE Is Attracting, Developing, and Retaining Global Talent. *Harvard Business Review*, February 8, 2012.

Turley, Jim. Why Business Needs Women—and Women Need Male Allies. Catalyst blog post, September 9, 2013.

Endnotes

[i] Education and Synthetic Work-Life Earnings Estimates, American Community Survey Reports, U.S. Census Bureau, 2011.

[ii] Bureau of Labor Statistics, 2013 Earnings and Unemployment Rates by Educational Attainment, March 2014.

[iii] Graduate-Degree Jobs With $100K Salaries, *US News & World Report*, March 11, 2011.

[iv] Civilian labor force by sex, 1970 – 2012, Bureau of Labor Statistics, Current Population Survey. Graph by the Women's Bureau, U.S. Department of Labor.

[v] Catalyst. *Pyramid: Women in S&P 500 Companies*. New York: Catalyst, January 13, 2015.

[vi] Victory over Rutgers shows Louisville football's Cards are a tough bunch of birds. C.L. Brown, *The Courier-Journal*, November 30, 2012.